Dr. Schweitzer playing the organ at Günsbach, Alsace, 1951

ALL MEN
ARE BROTHERS

A PORTRAIT OF *Albert Schweitzer*

By CHARLIE MAY SIMON

Photographs by ERICA ANDERSON

E. P. DUTTON & COMPANY, INC.

NEW YORK

Quotations at chapter beginnings are used with the permission of:

The Macmillan Company, New York, from: *Memoirs of Childhood and Youth,* © 1949; *The Philosophy of Civilization,* © 1949; *The Quest of the Historical Jesus,* © 1948.

Henry Holt and Company, Inc., New York, from: *Indian Thought and Its Development,* © 1936; *Out of My Life and Thought,* © 1949.

Acknowledgment

I wish to express my sincere gratitude to Dr. Albert Schweitzer and to the members of his staff for the hospitality shown me at Günsbach and at the Hospital of Lambaréné, and for the help and encouragement they have given me in writing this book.

List of Illustrations

ALL MEN ARE BROTHERS

A PORTRAIT OF Albert Schweitzer

Introduction

WHEREVER THE QUESTION IS ASKED: "Who is the greatest living person in the world today?" the answer is the same, with few exceptions. Albert Schweitzer. But if you should want to call on him, unless he happens to be on one of his rare visits to his home in France, you must go to the remote jungles of Africa, close to the Equator. And even in this day of jet-propelled planes, you would have to travel the last two and a half miles in a dugout canoe, or a small rowboat.

It was late in the afternoon when I arrived on my first visit to the hospital at Lambaréné. I had gone by plane as far as I could. The little local plane that flies from Brazzaville through the interior of French Equatorial Africa came to a landing in a bumpy, muddy field, with nothing but a hut and a tall stepladder to show it was a landing strip. From there I went by truck, over a trail that could scarcely be called a road, to the river landing where a rowboat was waiting to take me to the hospital. Five men were at the oars, and I knew by the clean bandages on their arms and legs that they were patients. And some instinct told me they were lepers, almost healed but kept on for observation.

We rowed for about an hour up the river against the current. The rainy season was on and the water was high. The muddy river stretched out in channels like arms around an island. Tall trees, the immense kapok with its gray smooth trunk and folds of ingrown roots, and the round umbrella-like mangoes grew at the edge of the banks, with their heavy branches dipping so low they touched the water. Flowering vines were twisted and tangled around them so that they seemed a part of the trees themselves. And I gave them names in my mind of the flowers at home they most resembled. One was slightly like a dogwood and another like a red camellia, and one had petals like the morning-glory. Small islands of grass and papyrus seemed to undulate with the waves like a tawny cat stretching its muscles. And here and there, on the fringed tops, a nest of grass swayed, a cradle for the water birds inside.

We pulled up to the landing, where I saw familiar faces among those waiting there to greet me. There was Mlle. Emma and Mlle. Mathilda. And there was Dr. Schweitzer himself. I recognized them at once from their photographs. And the warmth of their welcome gave me the feeling that I was with old friends, returning to a place I had known and loved.

Everything was so exactly as I had pictured it in my mind after reading the books by Dr. Schweitzer describing his jungle hospital that I felt at home at once in the little guest room that was mine. It was small but uncluttered, and two walls were open, with nothing more than screens and lattice that brought the whole outdoors into the room, with its view of the Ogowe and the long low banks beyond. On the table there was a tea tray with a pot of hot tea, sugar, a plate of cookies and a bowl of tangerines and bananas. And when I had had time to change to fresher clothes, the doctor came to pay a call of welcome, with Mlle. Emma who interpreted for us.

There was a simplicity about him that one finds only in the truly great. In spite of the heavy demands on his time, he puts up no barrier between himself and others. He might have been someone I had known all my life, though we spoke in different languages, with Mlle. Emma repeating after us sentence by sentence in German or English.

Quite against my will I became a patient at the hospital as

well as a visitor. A bicycle accident in Holland a few days earlier had resulted in a sprained ankle, which I was trying to ignore. But Dr. Schweitzer, with his keen, observing eye, was not deceived. He had one of his assistants bandage it, and I was kept in bed for several days. I might have been impatient at this idleness forced upon me, as any well person would be, if I had not had the daily visits of Dr. Schweitzer. He came with Mlle. Emma or with the nurse Mlle. Ali who changed the bandages, and through them he talked to me. He spoke of Goethe and compared his version of *Faust* with the older English one. And he asked me questions about America. He told of his one visit when he gave the lecture on Goethe at Aspen, Colorado. There was a twinkle in his hazel eyes when he described his bewilderment at the many push buttons in his compartment on the train.

"I pushed one button, thinking I was ringing for the porter," he said. "But instead something opened out into a bed. Then I pushed another button, for I needed the porter more than ever. And a washbasin appeared before my eyes."

He talked about the beauty of the river which I could see from where I sat propped in bed. And he talked about the people of Africa, with compassion and affection. It's strange how, as I recall these visits, the English words of the nurses are not the ones that come back to my memory. Instead, the doctor's intonation, his gestures, smiles and the expression of sympathy in his eyes remain with me. It is as though I had understood all he said without the need of words.

When I was up and able to walk again, the doctor knocked at my door one morning and motioned for me to take my helmet and come with him. We had no interpreter, so we walked in silence that morning. Our path lay through the citrus grove which they call the plantation. Ripening grapefruit, tangerines and limes hung on the trees like green-gold balls. Now and then the doctor paused to examine one that was gnarled with age and bore little fruit, then we walked silently on again. He picked a ripe orange and peeled it with a knife, then gave me half and ate the rest himself. Our walk ended at the pen of a baby antelope which had been brought in, orphaned by a hunter's gun. It came to put its moist nose against the wire and licked our hands for the salt. Again, in looking back, this walk in silence becomes more vivid in my mind than many a long conversation I have had with friends.

The days that followed were full. I went about alone on little journeys of exploration about the hospital grounds, for the doctors and nurses on the staff were busy every hour of the day.

On my first walk up the hill to the leper village, with Pierre, a little, languid-eyed leper boy as my guide, I thought of those two ancient fears as old as the history of man, serpents and lepers. We saw a palm branch sway though there was no breeze, and when the boy stopped in his tracks I knew it was from caution, because a mamba or a python might be hidden there. But it was only a palm rat that scurried across to another branch.

When I saw the patients come up to have their bandages changed and to take the pill and white powder, swallowed down with water, I knew that eventually every one would return home cured, thanks to the modern drugs and the hospital built here for them.

It was the time for the leper children to go to school. The Pahouin schoolmaster, dressed in white shorts and a white jacket, walked calmly along the hilly, narrow path that led to the schoolroom. If he took any notice of the way the children were trying to escape, some running off in one direction and some another, he gave no sign of it. But Mama Helene, the old Negro woman who mothers them all, followed in the rear, rounding them up. She ran, scolding, from one side to the other like a sheep dog, as she brought them into line. Was school as bad as that, I wondered, that they went so reluctantly? But when I saw how patient and sympathetic the Pahouin teacher was with them, I knew that it was only because they didn't like to be confined indoors for lessons when play was much more fun.

I had brought toy balloons as gifts for them, and I showed them how to blow them up and tie them with a string to hold the air. On the following Sunday afternoon, the children returned my visit, to serenade me while I had tea with the staff in the dining hall. With the teacher and Madame Helene directing them, they sang hymns in French and in their own tongue, giving to both the same intonation so that I could scarcely tell which was which. And then they presented me with gifts. There was a washbowl of squash and eggs and papayas and a tin pan of pistachio nuts. And there were several bunches of wild flowers gathered along the way and held out to me, clutched in little sweaty fists. What could I give to them, I wondered. It would not be fair to give to one unless I gave to all. A necklace I was wearing solved the problem. It was of large white beads, and I broke the string and gave each one a bead. Some of the smaller ones thought they were pills and started to put them in their mouths until I made a sign to them to put them on a string around their neck as I had done.

Often in the night there came the sound of music as the doctor, alone in his room, practiced on his metal-lined piano. Twice I was invited to sit beside him as he practiced. A Norwegian newspaperman, also a visitor at the time, sat on one side of the long piano bench with him and I on the other. And I think the doctor forgot immediately afterward that anyone at all was in the room with him as he went over and over a single passage of Bach until he had the fingering and timing that he wanted. He penciled it on the music sheet and then went on until he reached another passage which he wanted to perfect. After an hour he turned to us, as if suddenly realizing we were there.

"But I'm afraid I've been boring you," he said.

We both assured him we had felt it a privilege to be there. The Norwegian spoke in German and I in English, which the doctor understood, though the words themselves may not have been familiar.

"Do you play?" he asked me.

I, who had had to be coaxed and bribed and spanked to go near the piano when I was a child to practice the simple little pieces, could now feel shame before one who had made the best of all his potentialities; one who had never given in to a thought that a thing was too difficult to strive for.

Dr. Schweitzer played then for our pleasure and his own, until curfew time, when the bell was rung for silence on the hospital grounds so the patients might sleep. He took a lamp to light us on our way, and we stopped a moment to visit with the little antelope in its pen in a room adjoining the doctor's own. When we went out on the screened porch the pelican that came each night to roost on the rafters above his door flew off to a mango tree to wait until we had gone. Theckla the wild boar, and the fourth to bear the name, was restless in her box of straw outside the door. The doctor, holding the lamp in one hand, reached down to stroke her with the other. And, with that twinkle in his eye that could come so quickly, he began to sing Brahms's Lullaby and we joined in softly. The vicious-looking hog gave a contented grunt and closed her eyes, and we left her. The Norwegian and I went out in the soft tropical night, each to our own room, taking with us thoughts of a night to be remembered long afterward.

The table in the doctor's room had been piled high with papers, and we knew that, once alone, he would begin his work of answering letters or writing on his book. And even when the windows of his room were dark at last, his work of the day might not yet be over. His ear must ever be alert for sounds of footsteps on the path, bringing him a message that someone was in need of an emergency operation or a patient who had seemed to be improving had taken a turn for the worse.

It was almost midnight when I witnessed an operation being performed. A man had been brought in from some remote village far in the interior. I saw the look of fright on his face as he was wheeled into the operating room, for this was something so different from the grass huts that he had known, with no more furniture than squat stools of wood and sleeping mats woven from straw. His face also expressed the pain he felt, and beads of perspiration stood out on his forehead. One of the nurses knelt beside him and wiped his brow, talking to him in gentle, soothing words. She spoke in French which he could not understand, but there was something in the tone of her voice that comforted him, I know, for when it was time for the anesthetic to be given, he seemed more relaxed than when they had first brought him in.

I spent two weeks on that visit with Dr. Schweitzer at his hospital. It was with reluctance that I left, for I had begun to feel a part of the group of people and the work they did. As I sat at the long table with the doctor and his assistants for my last supper there, I felt a nostalgia for the place at the thought of leaving it. I looked at the faces of those about me, with the soft light of the oil lamps shining on them. I was deeply touched by the thought that all of them had come here, as the doctor had, out of compassion for others less fortunate. Some had been here many years, others had come recently and would soon return to their homes to take up another pattern of life. But the urge to help those in need of them was common to them all and was the reason for their being here.

The meal was simple: food grown on the place, with a few exceptions such as cheese for the noodles and sugar in the fruit compote. When we had finished, Dr. Schweitzer went to the piano and played the accompaniment for the hymns we sang. Then he returned to his place and read a passage from the Bible. I knew from a word here and there which I could recognize that they were the words of Paul. "And now abideth faith, hope, charity, these three; but the greatest of these is charity."

The next morning I stepped in the little rowboat and we started down the river toward the landing field. I turned for one last look and saw the doctor, with several of the staff, still standing on the bank to wave me out of sight. And I hoped with all my heart I could return some day and see them all again.

Before returning to America, I stopped off at the quiet little village of Günsbach, where I was a guest for several days at Dr. Schweitzer's home. I found the same simplicity here that I had found at his place in Africa. The rooms were uncluttered, and the furniture was comfortable but not luxurious. There were reminders of Africa throughout the house, in photographs and paintings and African carvings, just as in the doctor's room at his hospital there were paintings and photographs of his Alsatian home. And I knew that his heart was divided between these places he would always call home.

Two years later I went back to Alsace and to Africa, to write this book about a great man and the work he has done. Günsbach was not the quiet little village I had seen before, for Dr. Schweitzer was there on one of his visits from Lambaréné. Automobiles and motorcycles and taxicabs were parked outside the door, and a stream of people was constantly coming in and out, for the doctor would turn no one away.

I saw him on my birthday, and when I asked his permission to write this book about him for the young people of my country, he didn't know that his consent was my most cherished birthday gift. I began writing in Colmar, and returned from time to time to Günsbach. As I walked the road to Münster that he had walked as a boy, or watched the red-cheeked children playing in the schoolyards and the village square the same games he had played long ago, it seemed to me at times that I, too, had been a child growing up in Alsace. In my fancy I had climbed those hills on a summer day and had coasted down them on a bobsled when snow was on the ground. And it seemed I had sat long hours in a room, cluttered with dark and heavy furniture, studying or practicing on the piano.

When I had finished the part of the book that tells of Dr. Schweitzer's childhood and youth, I returned then to the hospital at Lambaréné to write of his work in Africa. Mlle. Varena met me in the rowboat and with her were the leper oarsmen. With the exception of two, they were not the same ones who had rowed me up the river two years before. Those men had been completely cured and had returned to their villages to take up their old life again. And the ones who had taken their places in the boat were far on their way to recovery, too.

It is like coming home again to find myself in the little guest room that had been mine before. Outside the screened wall I can look out on the beautiful Ogowe. Half-naked, laughing Negro children play in the shade of the mango tree that grows close to the house. One starts to sing and the others take it up, chanting in a tomtom kind of rhythm. *Aie boi la na. Aie boi la na.* Fritzi, the tame chimpanzee, orphaned by a hunter's gun and brought to the hospital to be raised, tries to join in, and the children scream with pretended fright, and with shouts of laughter at the same time.

I find myself comparing this scene, not so much with the familiar surroundings of my own home, but with Alsace, from where I have lately come. I think of the clear skies and clean, crisp air, of vineyards, and neat farmhouses, and gardens where vegetables and flowers grow side by side. Two wars have been fought over this land in my lifetime, and another, still bitterer one was fought a generation earlier. It seems fitting to me that from a place that has been made a battle-ground against its will so many times, there should have come one whose compassion and reverence for life has given us new faith and a goal to try to reach.

Chapter I

Not one of us knows what effect his life produces, and what he gives to others. That is hidden from us and must remain so, though we are often allowed to see some little fraction of it so that we may not lose courage.

Memoirs of Childhood and Youth

THE PEOPLE of Alsace call their land a serene and smiling place, though wars have been fought for its possession since the time, two thousand years ago, when Julius Caesar came up from the south, leading his well-trained legions into battle against the Germans, invading from the north. Later Charlemagne's grandsons waged war against each other for this same land. And from time to time, all through the years, armies have marched in from one direction and another, from Sweden and from Spain, from Italy, Hungary, Germany and from France itself. Each laid claim to the place and to the people, fighting first with spears and bows and arrows, and then with guns, cannons and bombs.

In the summer of 1870 there came again that familiar sound of soldiers' feet marching into Alsace. Guns boomed and cannons roared, until at last the white flag of surrender was raised on the spire of the Cathedral of Strasbourg. This time the Prussians were the conquerors, and Alsace was taken from the French and made part of the German Empire.

The Alsatians are a proud and stubborn race and, no matter which country claims them, they have a fierce loyalty to their own soil. When the war was over, they set about clearing away the debris. They repaired the damage done to their

houses, and they plowed their fields and planted their vineyards again in neat, even rows. Theirs was a land so rich and
abundant that it was small wonder that other nations wanted
it and so often fought over it. The wheat granary, the bread
basket, the wine cellar of the world, it was called.

"Whatever you find elsewhere, you'll find three times as
much in Alsace," the people like to say.

They sing a song so old that no one knows its origin.

> Three castles on one mountain,
> Three churches to one graveyard,
> Three cities in one valley,
> Three stoves for one room.
> That is our Alsace!

There came again an air of repose, and the people went on
with their own way of life as they had done after every war.
They met at the village fountains, at the cafés and in the
churches, and they spoke the language they had always
spoken. It was a soft and gentle kind of German with many
French words added to make it richer, for they knew both
languages well.

Five years passed, and the people could once more call their
land a serene and smiling place. The year 1875 was a year of
peace and promise.

"A good year for the vineyards," the winemakers said.

The grapes were plump and sound. And the fields were
green with growing wheat, waving and rippling in the wind
like the waters of the river Fecht as it flowed through the
Münster Valley. The war was no more than a memory now,
living only in the stories told beside the fire on a winter evening, or during the long summer twilight.

There were many who remembered the young Pastor
Albert Schillinger of Strasbourg, and they liked to tell about
how he had gone to Paris to bring back medical supplies for

the people under siege. The Germans surrounding the city captured him upon his return and held him prisoner, but the medicine he had with him was allowed to go through, and many lives were saved because of it.

"I would not be alive today except for him," one old woman was fond of saying. "When the siege was over and milk was scarce, it was Pastor Albert Schillinger who came every day to bring his own allowance to me."

Albert Schillinger's sister Adele listened proudly to these stories. She was married to Louis Schweitzer, also a pastor, and when their son was born she named him Albert, in memory of her beloved brother who had died three years before.

The child was thin and frail, and often as she held him in her arms and sang soft lullabies to him Adele Schweitzer must have wondered how much longer she would have him with her. From her window in the little house at Kaisersburg, the house with the turret, at the upper end of the village street, she could hear the shouts and laughter of children at their games. And she pressed her son closer to her, with a silent prayer that he would grow as strong and rosy-cheeked as they, and laugh and play the way they were doing now.

In the early summer of 1875, when Albert was six months old, his father was called as pastor to the church at Günsbach, a small village beside the Fecht River in the Münster Valley of Alsace.

People came from all the neighboring villages to welcome the new pastor and his little family. The village men took off their wooden *sabots* and put on leather shoes, and they wore their Sunday suits and broad-brimmed black hats. The women wore dark shawls brightened with flowery designs worked into the cloth, and they tied their prettiest aprons over their long, full skirts.

Adele Schweitzer stood beside her husband in the parlor of the manse to meet the new parishioners and the pastors of the villages close by who had come with their wives. In her arms she held the baby Albert, dressed for the occasion in a long white dress gaily trimmed with lace and tucks and colored ribbon bows. And the daughter Louise, in a pretty new dress also, stood close to her mother's skirts.

The wives of the neighboring pastors came up, one by one, to greet the newcomers. They patted the head of the little girl, still scarcely more than a baby herself. Then they looked at the child in his mother's arms, ready to make some pleasant compliment about how fine and healthy he was, or how pretty for a boy. But when they saw him, so pale and thin he seemed scarcely able to breathe, they stopped short in embarrassment, groping for something polite that they could say.

The young mother stood it as long as she could. Then, suddenly, with her child held closer to her, she ran to her bedroom and cried softly to herself.

It might have been the good air of Günsbach, or the fresh, wholesome milk from neighbor Leopold's cow, but it was also through a mother's prayers and desperate determination that the child began to grow stronger and healthier from that time on. He learned to crawl and then to walk and run pattering over the floors of the old manse, as plump and rosy-cheeked as any child in Alsace.

When he was still in petticoats, too small to go beyond the fence to play, this manse was his world. The house was over a century old, and the yard, small to the eyes of a grownup, seemed immense to little Albert. There was always some new wonder to explore; snow on the ground in winter, or red roses hanging heavy in the heat of a summer day. The steady, sleepy tick-tock of an old clock, a procession of ants marching in the path in close formation. Everywhere he turned, there was something to hold the attention of a small child. He sat on a stool in the yard and looked on, while his father took honey from the wooden hives, and when one of the pretty winged creatures settled on his hand and crawled about, he laughed with delight. But soon enough his laughter turned to a shriek of pain that brought the whole family around him.

He was taken up and comforted and petted, and the hand the bee had stung was kissed to take the pain away. It was nice to have all this affection and attention. Tears that had started because of the sting and the disappointment that the little creature he had so admired had betrayed him fell now because he wanted this attention to continue. But even as he cried, with no tears left in his eyes, he felt the remorse a sensitive child will feel, for he knew full well he was deliberately misbehaving.

As the months passed, the boy's world grew to take in the whole village with its houses and its people, and the small orchards, vineyards and vegetable patches on the outskirts, which the villagers owned and tended. And the center of Albert's expanding universe was the church where his father preached, with its steeple that towered so high it could be seen above all the roofs. At times it seemed to dwarf even the very mountains in the distance.

The church bells rang early on Sunday mornings, and the first call was for the Catholic service. When this was over, the sexton Jaegle rang the bells again. Then the Protestants came to worship in their way, here in the same church.

From the time he was three years old, Albert was taken to church and allowed to sit in the pew with the grownups. It was something to look forward to the whole week through. He was dressed in his Sunday clothes and he wore his leather shoes. The servant girl, sometimes tender and affectionate and sometimes scolding good-naturedly in her Alsatian way, washed him and brushed his hair.

"Oh, your hair!" she would exclaim, brushing so hard his scalp fairly tingled, as she tried to make it stay in place. "Unruly within, unruly without. The way your hair grows shows how unruly you are inside."

Was it true, he wondered. Was he really unruly inside, like the hair on his head that wouldn't stay in place, no matter how hard or how long it was brushed, no matter how much brilliantine the servant girl rubbed on it? Five minutes later it was always sure to blow and fall in all directions, and before he even had time to reach the church, it was so tousled there was nothing left of the part so carefully made.

Albert removed his cap when he went inside and took his place on the bench between his mother and the servant girl. Something of the solemnity and devotion of the people there, dressed in the somber black costume of the region, was felt also by the child and became a part of him long before he could understand the meaning of the services.

It seemed to him there was nothing in all the world so fine as the Catholic chancel facing him, with its altar painted to look like gold. There were vases on it filled with artificial flowers, looking as fresh, winter and summer, as flowers growing in a garden. And there were metal candlesticks with tall candles, magnificent even though their lights had been extinguished for the simpler Protestant services. On the wall above the altar, with the light from the two windows shining softly on them, were two large gilt statues of Joseph and the Virgin Mary, seeming to look down and give a blessing to the whole congregation. Beyond them, through the windows, one could see the shapes of trees and the roofs of houses weathered by centuries into many shades of red, like Joseph's coat of many colors. And beyond that, the eye could travel on to white clouds floating lazily in a blue sky that reached far out into infinity.

When hymns were sung the small boy joined in, singing loudly the words he knew, but if he raised his voice too high he was sure to feel the gloved hand of the servant girl clasped over his mouth. If he yawned ever so slightly, the same thing was sure to happen. But when he saw his father get up to take his place in the pulpit, he sat so still the servant girl could keep her cotton-gloved hands folded quietly in her lap throughout the sermon.

God seemed close and intimate then, with Albert's father preaching in the same quiet, simple way a man would talk in his home. And the devil, too, could seem real to a serious child. A mysterious face, as shaggy as the devil's own face must have been, appeared from time to time during the services. It looked down from a bright frame beside the organ every time the people stood to sing the hymns. But when the pastor prayed and when he preached the sermon, the face disappeared. Now, who but the devil himself would do a thing like that, the small boy thought. And it all went to show what a coward the devil was, for when the Word of God was spoken he disappeared.

It was not until Albert was older that he came to recognize the face as that of Daddy Iltis, the organist, looking in a mirror to see when it was time to start or stop playing the accompaniment to the familiar hymns.

The people of the Bible also seemed close and intimate to Albert. Abraham and Moses and Simon Peter and the apostle Paul were as alive in his thoughts as his playmates, George and Henry and Fritz. He sat solemnly listening to his father tell about them, and thoughts strange for a child ran through his head. There were many things he wondered about and even then he had a way of always asking the reason why. He thought of the Three Wise Men from the East bringing gold and myrrh and frankincense to the infant Jesus in his bed of straw. With gifts as rich as these, how could Joseph and Mary ever be poor again? What happened to the Wise Men afterward? Did they ever come back? And if they did, why was there no more mention of them? And there were the shepherds who heard the angels sing that night, of peace on earth and good will toward men. Why hadn't they stayed on to follow Jesus and become disciples, along with the twelve who were chosen in later years?

In the family Bible there was a picture of Moses, shown with horns on his head, that set the boy to wondering. Albert put his hand on his own forehead and it seemed to him he could feel two bumps where horns might appear any day. What an awful thing to happen to a person! It was something to worry about in secret for many a day. Every time he put his hand to his forehead, hoping he had been mistaken, there was the fresh torment of finding the bumps still there. And old Jaegle must have noticed something, too, for he had begun to tease about it.

Every Sunday morning after the bells were rung for the Protestant services, the sexton came to the manse to ask the numbers of the hymns to be sung and to get the things needed for baptisms, if there were to be any. Solemnly he wiped his shoes and solemnly he rang the doorbell. Albert was always there beside the door when it was opened, longing desperately to run away and hide, yet held there, unable to move in spite of himself, staring in the way a bird might stare at a snake. The same thing happened every time. With his true Alsatian wit, without a smile or change of expression, the old man made a grab at the boy's forehead.

"Ah, yes," he would say solemnly. "The horns are growing all right."

This went on until one day Albert went to his father with the pages of the Bible turned to the picture of Moses.

"Can other people have horns, too?" he asked.

His father's answer put his mind at rest. Only Moses was pictured in such a way, he was assured, and horns would not grow on people's foreheads. Now Albert no longer took the sexton's teasing seriously. Instead, he could laugh about it, so that the old man had to search his mind for something else to tease a small boy about.

Not only were the people of the Bible as close to Albert as the Günsbach neighbors, but the places mentioned there were as familiar as any of the villages of Alsace.

The Hohneck Mountain could be seen from the village, towering high above all the other mountains that closed around the Münster Valley. Mount Ararat might have been just such a place as this, when Noah landed his ark there and turned the animals out. The rainbow that spread before Noah as a promise would have been as clear and bright as the rainbows over the Hohneck. And there would have been the same shining raindrops on the bushes and the same mud in the pathway such as lingered after every rain at Günsbach.

One wet summer when Albert was kept indoors for days on end because of the constant rain, he thought of the flood of Noah's time. He had heard his father read the story aloud so many times that it came back to his mind like the words of a song.

> And the flood was forty days upon the earth;
> and the waters increased and bare upon the
> ark, and it was lifted up above the earth.
> And the waters prevailed exceedingly upon
> the earth; and all the high hills that were
> under the whole heaven were covered.
> Fifteen cubits upward did the waters prevail;
> and the mountains were covered.

Surely it had been raining as much as forty days and forty nights at Günsbach. But the waters hadn't even come up to the houses, let alone cover all the high hills or the mountains that were under the whole heaven.

Again there was the question "Why?" And his father gave the answer to a child's troubled question.

"Well, you see, at that time, in the beginning of the world, it didn't just rain in drops the way it does now. It was more like water pouring out of buckets."

Albert took his father's words seriously, and afterward, when he heard the story of Noah and his ark, he wanted it all told, even to the way the rain poured from the heavens like water from buckets.

As the boy grew, the world he knew grew with him. He could name the hills rising on both sides of the valley, the tall peak of the Hohneck and the chains of the Schlucht that seemed to come closer or to recede in the distance with each change of light. And he knew that the river Fecht, sparkling and singing its way through the valley, had its source high in the wooded mountain, and that it flowed on to join the waters of the Ill, then on to the Rhine itself.

He knew that beyond France and Germany there was a wide ocean. And across the Channel, there was a place called England and north of that was Scotland. His mother, reading the novels of Sir Walter Scott, sometimes dreamed and talked of going there with the family for a visit, so they could see the country for themselves. Far beyond the oceans there were other countries, America, China, Australia.

Every spring the storks came to Günsbach. They could be seen, vivid in their black and white plumage, nesting on the chimneytops or stalking on long red legs, with their quiet air of dignity as they searched for frogs beside the riverbanks. And in the first cool days of late summer, they flew away to far-off Africa. The noisy little cuckoo, searching for a hedge sparrow's nest to steal and lay her eggs in, spent her winters in Africa, too.

Albert heard more about this little-known land from a book which his father read aloud during the Sunday afternoon services at the church. He sat still in the pew listening while his father read the words in the same quiet, gentle way he had of talking in their own home. The book was the memoirs of a missionary named Casalis who had gone to Africa. He wrote of the dark, mysterious jungles where no white man had ever gone before. The tales he told would impress any boy, tales of elephants and monkeys and leopards crouched in trees ready to spring down on a passer-by. But even more impressive were the stories of the people living there, and their pitiful need.

"You see our distress," Pastor Louis Schweitzer translated the words from the French for his congregation. "You are able to help us and you have promised to do so. Stay here and teach us. We will promise to do all that you wish. Our sorrows are like the raging river. Wait. The flood will pass. You will stay."

Chapter II

The traveler on the plain sees from afar the distant range of mountains. Then he loses sight of them again. His way winds slowly upwards through the valleys, drawing ever nearer to the peaks, until at last, at a turn of the path, they stand before him, not in the shapes which they had seemed to take from the distant plain, but in their actual forms.

Quest of the Historical Jesus

ALBERT SCHWEITZER's first glimpse of the world outside was when he was taken to visit his godmother Barth, who lived in Colmar, a half-day's journey away by coach and carriage. As cities go, Colmar is quite small, but it was an exciting, dazzling place for a boy who had known only the quiet little village of Günsbach. His eyes couldn't take in enough of all the strange, new sights. There were more people coming and going along the narrow sidewalks than he had ever seen at one time before, and the streets were crowded with carts and carriages and men on horseback. On market days there was as much activity as at a Günsbach Fair, with booths and stalls set up in the Square beside the Cathedral and along the sidewalks surrounding it. Lengths of colored cloth and sheets and tablecloths, on display to sell, floated in the breeze like gay banners everywhere he turned. And in the Square of Fruit Markets, there were baskets of cherries and currants, or ripe red apples and golden pears.

Some of the shops and houses of Colmar were old even when Columbus discovered the New World across the Atlantic. Huge beams of timber, weathered dark with age,

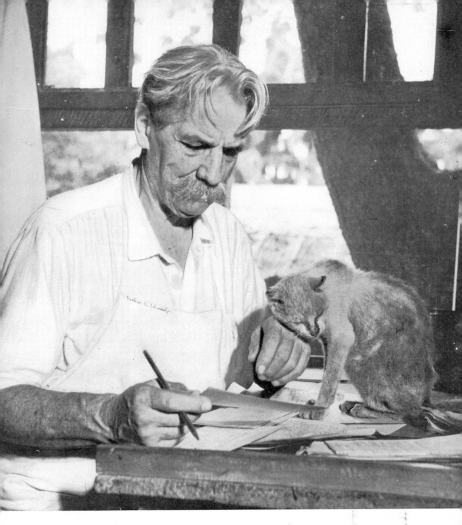

With Sisi at his desk in the consultation room in Lambaréné

showed through the plaster of the sharply pointed gables, forming uneven patterns that made the houses seem to lean against each other for support. And the high, steep roofs of tile were moss-grown with the years. In the evening, when the streets were a little quieter, the houses caught the glow of the setting sun, with the colors blending on the old walls and roofs and on the green painted shutters and the bright red geraniums in pots on the window sills. It was then, with the bells of St. Martin's chiming, their many tones mingling high and low and reverberating through the streets, that the city seemed to slip back into a past long forgotten. It was like stepping into the pages of a picture book to walk along the winding, cobbled streets, with corners that turned suddenly as if there were some surprise in store, always just a little out of sight. The sidewalks, paved with small squares of brick laid in fan-shaped patterns, were well worn with five hundred years of footsteps that had walked that way.

The people of Colmar took pride in the rich legacy of their past. On Sunday afternoons and on holidays, they strolled past the many statues in the parks and squares, and the Museum was crowded with those who came to look again and again at the paintings and sculpture of long ago.

Thursday was visiting day in Albert Schweitzer's childhood. When guests came from the neighboring villages to visit the Barths, they were always taken to the Museum after the ample noon meal was over. When Albert was there, he was allowed to go along with them. Everywhere he turned there was something to catch his eye, tempting him to lag behind. There were wood carvings worked with great care down to the smallest detail of a leaf, or a wrinkle in an old man's face. And there was a wooden statue of Christ on a donkey no bigger than a child's hobby horse. It was on a platform with wheels, for it had been used in processional parades long years ago. But the place where Albert Schweitzer could always be found after the others had moved on was where the paintings of Grünewald were hung.

There were pictures of "St. Paul the Hermit" and of "St. Anthony's Temptations," with landscapes that might have been in Alsace, and yet with trees and rocks that took weird shapes, and demons and animals surrounding Anthony, painted with a realism that would hold any child in fascination.

Another painting by this same Alsatian master, who had lived four hundred years before, was of the child Jesus in His mother's arms, and this, too, was one of Albert's favorites. The painting showed a room like many a nursery room in Alsace, with the cradle and the baby clothes thrown carelessly over it, the chamber pot and the wooden tub with a towel across it. To the left a group of angels were playing musical instruments, and behind, where the room opened out to the blue of the night sky, there was God surrounded by a host of angels, in an aura of colors that seemed to sing with light. To the child there was nothing unnatural in this blending of realism and fancy. Such things might well be, he knew.

The painting he was to recall more vividly than all the others, however, was the one of Jesus on the Cross. The Mother Mary, in a flowing white veil, stood in a gesture of despair on one side, while the apostle John, in a robe the color of fire, bent down to comfort her. His straw-colored hair was as tousled as Albert's own, and as the child gazed at the picture before him, he wondered if the Apostle had been scolded, too, as he himself had so often been, and if he had had his hair brushed and slicked down time and again until his scalp stung with the strokes, only to have it rumple and fall in all directions immediately afterward. Perhaps there hadn't been anything to what the servant girl so often said, "Unruly within—unruly without." Hadn't John, with all his unruly hair, become one of the Apostles?

Albert came in time to know Colmar almost as well as he

34

knew his own village of Günsbach. His godmother Barth often came after him and took him home with her to stay for days at a time. And when one or both of the servant girls took him out for a walk, he learned the names of the streets they passed. They were the kind of names a child would love, such as Street of the Bears, Street of the Stork, Street of the Frog, and streets called Hunter, Baker, Merchant, Locksmith, and Fishermen.

On one memorable Sunday, Albert's godmother went to pay a call and left him in care of the two servant girls.

"Take the child out for a little walk," she said as she left. "But make it a short one, and be sure to keep a close watch over him."

As soon as she was out the door, the girls dressed up in their Sunday best and went out, with young Albert trotting between them. They walked along the winding street that turned this way and that, past little bakery shops and cafés where mustached or bearded men sat at tables out of doors, drinking Alsatian beer or good Rhine wine. There was a band playing in the distance, and it was there the girls chose to go. Soon they found themselves at the Horbourg Village Fair, where the young people were dancing the country dance of the region.

The servant girls joined in the dance, but at the same time they kept their promise to godmother Barth and kept a close watch over Albert. One took his right hand and the other his left. And each had, on her other side, a dashing young dancing partner. All afternoon they danced while the big brass horns played a lively tune, and the little boy with tousled hair between them, quickened his steps to keep up. Backward and forward and circling around, the child was enjoying himself as much as the girls and their escorts were. But when it was all over and they started on the long walk back home, there came again that conflict in the conscience of the sensitive child. Suppose godmother Barth should ask him where he had gone and what he did. He'd have to choose between telling a lie or being disloyal to the servant girls. He was tortured in his mind, trying to decide which it would be, but luckily he was spared.

"Did you have a good time?" was all his godmother asked.

And truthfully the boy could answer, "Yes."

Another time he didn't come off so well. It was when an older boy took him out for a walk. Frau Barth warned the boy as she had warned the servants to keep a close watch over the child and not to walk too far.

"And don't go in the direction of the river," she added.

The older boy promised, then, taking Albert by the hand, he led the way with sure steps as if he knew well where he was headed. They went along the narrow, crooked streets, past the Place of the Six Black Mountains, where there was a statue of a knight in armor, with sword and shield. Old Jaegle, the sexton, said he'd have to wear just such a suit of iron when he grew up. He knew now the old man was only teasing, just as he had teased about the horns. But he hadn't been too sure at first, for Jaegle had such a serious way of making jokes.

"You know we belong to Prussia now," he had said. And with that dignified air of his, and that way he had of saying a thing without a change of expression, he could make a person believe anything was true. "And in Prussia all the boys have to be soldiers. And soldiers wear suits of iron. You can see that in the picture books. Pretty soon now you'll have to go up to the blacksmith shop and let the blacksmith measure you for a suit of those iron clothes, too."

At first Albert was drawn to the blacksmith shop, waiting to see if there were any soldiers coming there to be measured for suits of iron. But now that he was older, he knew better. He knew that soldiers wore suits of cloth instead.

"Come on," the older boy said impatiently, when Albert lingered behind.

Dragging him along by the hand, he turned into the Street of the Fishermen. Suddenly, around the corner, they came upon the river Lauch.

The Lauch is larger than the river Fecht, but it is quiet, where the Fecht gurgles and roars constantly as it rushes over its stony bed. Albert stood beside his companion and looked down at the still water, with the soft pink and yellow of the old houses reflected as if in a mirror. Now and then a boat passed by, loaded to the waterline with vegetables from the nearby farms.

"Let's find a boat that's easy to unfasten," the older boy said.

Without even waiting for a reply, he scrambled down the banks and searched until he found a boat that was not properly tied. Albert watched him untie the boat and step in, and he longed with all his heart to join him, yet he hesitated.

"Come on," the boy said, motioning for him to get in, too.

"But remember what your mother said," Albert replied. "Remember what my godmother said."

The boy only stared as if he could not, for the life of him, understand why anyone should pay attention to what the grownups had to say. And Albert could resist the temptation no longer. Under the boy's stare he stepped into the boat. Off they went, gliding beneath the overhanging branches of the trees, passing other boats that came and went. The boy guided the boat with a skill that showed he had done this many times before. And what a wonderful time they had! It was easy to imagine that the still little river Lauch was a wide ocean, and the small boat was a sailing ship taking them off to lands far away.

The awakening came when angry voices were heard in the distance on the riverbank.

"We'd better go back now," the older boy said calmly.

They rowed back to find the owner of the boat standing on the bank in a furious rage.

"This time I won't let you off! This time I'm going to tell your mother on you," he said, shaking his finger at the two children.

When godmother Barth took young Albert back to his home at Günsbach, his mother asked if he had been a good boy.

"Well, not entirely," his godmother replied.

Though she explained that it was really the fault of the older boy, Albert was not spared punishment. But when it was all over and penance was done, there were still memories of a delightful ride in a boat down the river Lauch.

Like any boy, Albert often dreamed of what he would be when he grew up. When he was very small he saw the cowherds take the village cows up to the mountains where the grass was green, and he saw the swineherds going off to tend the village swine. What a wonderful life it must be, he thought, to spend all day on a mountaintop, running and playing as free as the wind, while the cattle grazed peacefully along the slopes. He would have to be a soldier first, of course. Old Jaegle was right in one thing. When he was older, since Alsace was now a part of Germany, he, like every other German boy, would have to serve some time in the Prussian army for military training. But after that was over, there were so many things a boy could dream of doing, so many adventures waiting in the future.

"I'm going to be a sailor," he once said to his mother.

"Sailors have to sleep on hammocks instead of soft goose feather beds like yours," his mother reminded him.

But sailors led a life that anyone in feather beds could envy, sailing over the seas to lands far away, America, the Orient, and down to Africa.

There was a statue in the park at Colmar, and Albert never tired of walking past it to stand before it, held in fascination. It was made by the Colmar sculptor Bartholdi, who was then in Paris working on the great Statue of Liberty, which was to be a gift from France to America. The statue he had made for his native town was also immense. There was a tall figure of the hero Admiral Bruat, and around the base there were huge figures to represent the four corners of the earth, Europe, America, Australia and Africa. This last, especially, caught the eye of Albert Schweitzer from the time he first saw it. It was the giant figure of a Negro in a half-reclining position. There was something melancholy about it, with the powerful, muscular body seeming to be on the point of rising up, yet with the head bowed down in sorrow. It was a figure that haunted the boy so that he could not shake it from his mind.

Chapter III

If I am a thinking being, I must regard other life than my own with equal reverence. For I shall know that it longs for fulness and development as deeply as I do myself.

Reverence for Life

THE LITTLE FAMILY GREW. Now there were three sisters, Louise, the oldest, then Adele and Margerit, and later there was a brother Paul. The walls of the old manse echoed with their chatter and songs and laughter.

Sometimes their father looked up briefly from his desk in a study that smelled of papers and old books. Then the scratching of his pen could be heard again, as he went on writing his sermon, or composing stories he called "The Village Tales," which were printed in the *Church Messenger*, and in calendars. If their mother tried to hush her children into silence, it was because she remembered her own childhood, when her father went off to his study to prepare his sermons. There had to be absolute silence all over the house in those days. No visitor had been admitted, and the children were allowed to talk only in whispers. Even her older brother who was away at school had not been allowed to return home on a holiday if it happened to fall on a Saturday.

Albert had never known his Grandfather Schillinger, but stories were still told in the valley about him. There were some who remembered how he would go outside the church when the Sunday services were over, and talk with the people gathered there about the latest political news or some new discovery of the human mind. He had a telescope which he liked to share with friends and neighbors, whenever there was anything of especial interest in the sky, such as falling stars or a planet coming closer to the earth. Yet he was stern and demanded respect. No man dared call upon him at the manse without wearing a black coat and the high hat of the period. And he had a temper that flared up quickly, though he could get over his anger just as quickly.

Albert had inherited this quick temper from his mother's father, which, try as he would, he could not easily control. And there was the same easy forgiveness and smile of good humor that always followed. He inherited, too, his Grandfather Schillinger's love of music. He was told of how his grandfather had improvised on the piano or organ harmonies of his own to suit his mood. So great had been his interest in organs that when he happened to go to a strange town where he had never been before, what he had always wanted to see first were the organs in the churches there. He was known to have spent whole days at a time in the chancel of a church, looking on while an organ was being built, following every phase of its construction.

The old square piano which he had played upon was now at the manse at Günsbach, and music had been a part of Albert Schweitzer's life as far back as he could remember. From the time he was five, barely large enough to reach the keys, his father started giving him lessons. Even then he had an ear for harmony, and when he had learned to play from notes, he was allowed to make up songs and hymn tunes of his own. At twilight, his father would come from his study and play, while the children listened. Often he improvised the melodies as he went along.

It was a happy home for a child to grow up in. There were picnics in the summer, when the whole family packed a lunch and walked up the slopes of the hills. They would come to the forest of oaks and chestnuts, where squirrels, safe on the high limbs, scolded down at them as they passed by, and where the hares hid behind clumps of whortleberries, as still as any stone until they were out of sight. Still higher, where the firs and pines and beeches grew, deer and the ferocious wild boar crept stealthily in the underbrush.

There was fun in winter, too, with rides in the big lumbering cart that belonged to the next-door neighbor. Or, when the ground was covered with ice and snow, there was skating, or coasting on sleds down the road behind the church.

All too soon this glorious freedom came to an end. It was time for Albert to start to school. With a new slate under his arm, he set out, reluctantly, with footsteps that lagged far behind as his father led the way. It was October, when the trees on the hillsides were gay in autumn colors, and in the valley the robins and bullfinches flitted here and there with the restlessness of any traveler, before starting off on their fall migration. And storks on the chimneytops were flapping their immense wings to practice for their long flight to Africa.

With all his heart Albert wanted to break away and run back to the manse, but he trudged on behind his father, past the village fountain where women chatted as they drew pitchers of water for their kitchens. Around the corner, not far from the river, there was the school, mysterious and forbidding to a child who had never been inside before. But once there, it was not as bad as he had imagined it would be.

Daddy Iltis, the organist, was one of the teachers. And there was Fräulein Goguel who taught the youngest children. She was all right once you came to know her, even though she could only pick out the tune with one finger when she played the accompaniment for their singing lesson, and not with the harmony in several parts as Albert could do even then. His classmates were village children he knew well. They played together at recess time and before and after school, running in and out among the linden trees, their wooden shoes clop-clopping on the hard, bare ground. They fought and quarreled as boys will do. But their quarrels were over quickly, followed by vows of friendship, and once again the fun and laughter began.

Albert Schweitzer was quick to laughter, and his classmates liked nothing better than to do or say something to make him laugh out loud in school. Yet underneath this gaity there was a sensitiveness and a feeling of deep sympathy for others that was to stay with him all through his life.

On his way home from school one day, he and another boy named George Nitschelm began to wrestle to test their strength. Though the other boy was older and bigger, Albert soon had him down.

"Yes, and if I could have meat broth like you have for supper twice a week, I'd be just as strong as you are," the boy said as he jerked himself out from under.

The words were like a blow to Albert, and he took no pleasure in winning the game. And the broth that was brought to the table in a steaming bowl that night lost its good flavor when he thought of George Nitschelm who had none.

He began to see his playmates with new eyes, these village boys with coarse, worn clothes and darned stockings and wooden shoes. For the first time he realized the difference in his own life and theirs, and he resented that difference. Since they wore wooden *sabots* every day and saved their leather boots for Sunday, then he would do the same. And he would not have gloves with fingers, for theirs had none. No matter how his parents coaxed or scolded and even punished him, he gave them no peace until he had his way. Even when an old coat of his father's was made over to fit him, he refused to wear it.

"Now you look like a regular little gentleman," the tailor had said when he was trying it on for a fitting.

If he thought this remark would please the boy, he was very much mistaken. Albert was determined from then on that he would never wear that overcoat. They could whip him or they could shut him up in the cellar, but he would hold out with all the Alsatian stubbornness which he had inherited from his Grandfather Schlissinger. And he did.

There was again the same stormy scene when he went with his mother to visit an elderly relative at Strasbourg. His mother took him to a shop that had boys' caps and hats to sell. One cap after another was brought for him to try on. Each one, the saleswoman assured his mother, was the latest fashion for small boys, but Albert wanted none of them. A sailor's cap was brought out, with ribbons dangling from it such as real sailors wore. This was the one his mother liked best, but Albert refused to keep it on his head.

"Then what kind of a cap *do* you want, you stubborn child?" the saleswoman asked in exasperation.

"I don't want any of these," he answered. "I want one like the boys at home wear."

The other saleswomen came up to see what all the commotion was about, then the manager came. At last a stock girl was sent back to another room, and she returned with a cap that had been put aside because no one wanted it. It was a rough, brown cap that could be pulled down over the ears, just such a cap as the village boys of Günsbach wore. Albert beamed with joy when he put it on. This was what he wanted. Now he would be like George and Henry and Fritz and all the other boys at school.

He expected his mother to scold when they left the shop. And he was sorry, as he always was after a burst of temper, feeling remorse that he had embarrassed his mother so before strangers. But to his surprise she said nothing. It was as if she knew in her heart he had some reason of his own for his behavior, and since she was not one to speak of things she felt deeply, she pretended to take no notice of it.

Sometimes his older sister Louise would take his part during some stormy scene, as if she, too, understood his struggle to be like the other boys. But his playmates little guessed the tears and punishment it cost him to dress and act as they did. They took no more notice of his wooden shoes and his gloves without fingers than they did of their own. But when there was the slightest quarrel such as boys at play will have, they never failed to say accusingly, "Oh well, after all you're one of the gentry."

There are thoughts that go on in a boy's mind that he does not talk about, even to his best friend, because he is not sure of being understood. Even when he was very small, Albert, when he said his prayers at night and asked God's blessing on those he knew and loved, his parents and sisters, his godmother Barth and godfather Louis, wondered why there should not be prayers for animals as well as for people. He thought of his dog Phylax and his neighbor's chestnut horse, the bees his father kept, the birds singing and nesting in the linden trees. He thought, too, of an old limping horse he had once seen in Colmar being led to the slaughterhouse, tugged forward by one man and beaten with a stick from behind by another. He made up a prayer of his own then and said it quietly to himself after he had said his spoken prayer aloud to his mother.

"Oh, Heavenly Father, protect and bless all things that have breath and keep them from harm, and let them sleep in peace tonight."

Thoughts that had been only vaguely felt before now began to take form in his mind. Every living creature on the earth and in the water and sky could feel pain as he could feel it, and all had the same joy of life and desire to live that he had.

There were times when he himself caused that pain, then he was tortured with remorse afterward. The brown dog Phylax was gentle enough when the children played and romped with him, but he became vicious at the very sight of a uniform, and had to be held in a corner every time the postman passed that way. Once he had even bitten a policeman. Albert tried to hold him back, but it was not always easy, with the dog barking and growling and baring his teeth in his struggle to break away. Sometimes he had to be punished with a switch to keep him quiet. A dog lives only for the moment, and when the postman had gone on his way Phylax became his gentle self again. But Albert, sitting afterward beside his dog, remembered how he had stood over him with the switch, and he thought of what he might have done. He needn't have acted so like a wild beast tamer, he told himself. He could just as easily have held the dog by the collar and stroked him, which would have quieted him just the same.

He would have the same regret after every ride in the neighbor's cart, when he had used the whip on the horse, old and asthmatic and tired from the day's work. He remembered the way the horse's flanks had worked with his hard breathing, and how tired his eyes seemed as he looked at him.

These were secret thoughts he kept to himself, which he dared not speak aloud, until one day in spring when he and his friend Henry Brasch were playing with slingshots which they had made.

"Come on, let's go up to the hill behind the church and shoot some birds," Henry said.

He led the way and Albert followed, not daring to refuse for fear he would be laughed at and teased.

It was near the end of Lent, and the valley was green with tender blades of new grass pushing up through the old. This hillside land behind the church was where the villagers had their orchards and vineyards and vegetable patches. The limbs of the trees were bare, but blossom buds were swelling, ready to burst into bloom on the first warm day. The birds flitted busily about, singing their song of early morning. The blackbird with its brilliant yellow bill and orange rings around its eyes set in the jet black of its feathers, sang its sweet liquid notes that rose and fell in the scale. The little bullfinch joined in, with a clear, piping call; then others took up the chorus, showing no fear of the boys as they came near.

Stooping like a red Indian hunter, Henry put a stone in the leather of his sling, ready to take aim, and he nodded to Albert to do the same.

Just at that moment the church bells began to ring, mingling their music with the song of the birds. Suddenly Albert threw down his slingshot and quickly began to shoo the birds away so they would be safe from his companion's stones. What did it matter if Henry did laugh at him! What did anything matter as long as he did what he felt in his heart was the right thing to do. The bells had been like a voice from Heaven then, and with their sound came thoughts of the commandment, "Thou shalt not kill."

This had taken more courage than any game of daring that boys might play. But now that he was no longer afraid of what other boys might think of him, he found that some of them understood and began to feel as he did about torturing or killing helpless animals. Twice he had gone fishing with rod and line in the river Fecht, because he was asked to do so. But he gave it up, because the sport lost its pleasure for him when he saw the worms put on the hook and the wrenching of the mouths of fishes that were caught.

Even then thoughts began to form in Albert Schweitzer's mind, though it was not until much later that he found words to express them. What right had he or anyone to kill or torture a living creature of whatever kind, if there was any way possible to keep from doing it. It was one thing, he knew, to kill a hawk that swooped down in a barnyard to snatch a helpless chicken, but it was something else to shoot a bird singing in a tree, only for the pleasure of killing. A farmer might cut down a thousand wild flowers in a meadow when he mowed hay to feed his stock. But if, on the way back to his house, he thoughtlessly switched off the head of a single blossom growing beside the road bank, he was needlessly injuring life.

When Albert was nine years old he left the village school and went to the school at Münster, two miles away. He walked the long way there and back alone, and it was during these walks that the feeling of kinship with nature grew stronger in him. He scarcely knew which season he liked best, for he began to feel himself a part of all.

The chestnut and cherry trees that grew in the deep ravine, shook their brown and yellow leaves in his path as he walked in the fall, and the vines were heavy with purple grapes. Then the snow fell, covering first the high peak of Hohneck like a jaunty white cap perched on a giant head, and spreading down into the valley later when the wind blew cold. In spring the cherry trees were covered with blossoms, as white as if the snow still lingered on them, and butterflies like snowflakes drifting in the breeze flew in and out among them. Robins and bullfinches and the little hedge sparrows busily built new nests or repaired old ones they had abandoned in the fall. And the voiceless storks clattered their long red beaks in a kind of chant.

The land rose sharply on one side and sloped down on the other to a meadow where scarlet poppies and blue cornflowers grew thickly through the grass in summertime. A dark line of trees ran through the valley, showing the course of the river as it sang and splashed over rocks as white as linen sheets in a tub.

The hills in the distance stood out like great waves rising

and falling, with their tops catching the sun and throwing their shadows in patches on the slopes. Sometimes a ragged cloud seemed caught by one, but it raveled out into another shape and drifted lazily away. In summer when the air was very still, one might almost think he heard the many tones of cowbells in the distance.

The little villages that nestled along the slopes could be seen clearly from the high road. Each had its church with a steeple rising high above the red-tiled roofs.

On one of the hills stood the ruins of an old castle, which could set a boy to dreaming of knights of old and stories read in history books of Charlemagne and of Adalrich, the first Duke of Alsace and his daughter the good St. Odele. There were tales told too of the wicked Count Rudolph who had lived in the castle of Hohlandsbourg eight hundred years ago, and had been the terror of the hills and valley. When he had not been at war, he had spent his time hunting, trampling down the peasants' crops with his horses and dogs, scattering their flocks of sheep and herds of cattle, and killing ruthlessly the roe and stag.

Once Albert tried to make a drawing of the castle, but he was not pleased with what he had done. And again he tried to make up lines of poetry to describe the things he saw on his walks each day to and from the Münster school. He was not satisfied with that either, and he knew that his gift was not for painting or for poetry. It was through music that he could best express his moods. Even now at nine, he was sometimes allowed to play the organ at the church services, taking the place of Daddy Iltis.

School closed in late June. It was the time when the linden trees in the schoolyard were in bloom, mingling into one all the smells of summertime, clover blossoms, new-mown hay, jasmine and honeysuckles on a fence row. And now the daily walks must come to an end.

49

All his life Albert would find it hard to break away from familiar and well-loved surroundings. It had been a happy year for him. The lessons themselves had not been easy, for in the beginning he was slow to learn. But the teachers had a way of giving him an interest in the subject. There was a Latin teacher to give him private instruction. And there was old Pastor Schaffer who put such feeling in the Bible stories he told that one could almost feel he was there to witness the happenings.

"I am Joseph, your brother, whom ye sold into Egypt." Tears came to the old man's eyes as he read.

Sobs could be heard among the pupils, too, as they heard of how Joseph fell on his brother Benjamin's neck and wept and Benjamin wept on his neck. And he kissed all his brothers and wept with them.

"Now therefore be not grieved or angry with yourselves that ye sold me hither, for God did send me to preserve life."

Albert was to remember long after how the old man's voice filled with emotion as he read.

It was decided that the boy would not return to Münster the following year. He would go instead to a larger school at Mulhouse, in the southern part of Alsace, where Greek and Latin were taught. It was two hours from Günsbach by train, and much too far to go home except for holidays. And Albert wished with all his heart he did not have to go.

Chapter IV

The ideas which determine our character and life are implanted in
mysterious fashion. When we are leaving childhood behind us,
they begin to shoot out. When we are seized by youth's enthusiasm
for the good and true, they burst into flower, and the fruit begins
to set.

Memoirs of Childhood and Youth

THE EIGHT YEARS AHEAD loomed like an eternity to Albert
Schweitzer on the day he left Günsbach to make his home in
Mulhouse. He should have felt grateful, he knew. His father,
trying to support a growing family on a pastor's small salary,
could never have afforded to send his son away to a secondary
school if it had not been for the generosity of his Uncle
Louis. He and his wife Sophie had no children of their own,
and they offered to take the boy to live with them until he
finished his education there.

Great-uncle Louis, also Albert's godfather, was director of
the elementary schools at Mulhouse, and he and his wife
made their home in the gloomy building of the Central
School. The city itself was gloomy enough with its mills and
factories, the first things to be seen from a train window, and
its shabby crowded tenements where the workers lived.

A homesickness came over the nine-year-old boy, and a
deep longing for the fun and laughter and the carefree life he
had had in his Günsbach home. He took even less interest in
his studies than he had before, whiling away his time in daydreams when he should have been listening to the teachers. It
was the same in the evenings when he returned to the home

of his uncle and aunt. They were stern and strict in their discipline, not only of him, but of themselves as well. The whole pattern of their lives was governed by a set of regulations, with every moment accounted for, from the time they got up in the morning until they went to bed at night. And they would not, under any circumstances, relax that schedule.

As soon as he finished eating breakfast, Albert had to go to the piano and practice until it was time to leave for school. The very fact that he had to do it made it work rather than the pleasure it had always been for him. And as soon as he returned home in the evening, there was homework to be done. It was the time of day when the year before he had been taking the quiet walk from Münster, pausing to watch a swallow skimming over the meadow or a butterfly hovering around a late aster, with smoldering pollen at its center. Three sisters and a brother, as well as his parents, were always waiting then to greet him, and his dog, dancing its little dog dance of welcome, with tail wagging joyously. Now instead, he must sit indoors at a table piled with schoolbooks and writing tablets, and struggle with some problem in mathematics or try to parse a Latin sentence. In spite of everything, his mind wandered off into daydreams then, as it did during his class periods at school.

He was aware of the sound of voices as the grownups talked softly together, his Great-uncle Louis and Aunt Sophie and the young woman who lived with them, a teacher at the girls' school. She was the daughter of Pastor Schaffer of Münster. It was that good old man who had given Albert the nickname of Isaac, which meant "laughter," because he was always quick to laugh. But here he was given no such name. In this house, where there were no other children but only stern and serious older people, there could be little fun and laughter.

Sometimes there came to Albert's ears the expression, "Ah, he's a man of ripe experience," as the older people talked of friends they knew. It was meant as a compliment, but to Albert there was something depressing about using the word "ripe" in such a way. Ripeness meant the end of growth. To him it was a time of dulled feeling and an end to ideals and enthusiasms. Why was it, he wondered, that if a grown man remembered and spoke at all of his early dreams, it was half laughingly, as if they were something to be ashamed of? Albert made a vow to himself then and there. He would never give up believing in justice and peace and kindness. All his life he would go on dreaming and planning and seeking these things. If growing ripe in experience meant an end to the ideals of youth and becoming half ashamed of them, then he wanted none of it.

There were fifteen minutes of glorious freedom each evening when it was time to set the table for supper and the books must be cleared away. Though he wasn't allowed to go outside and play, at least Albert was allowed to forget for a little while about Latin sentences and problems in mathematics, and read whatever he wanted. The first thing his hands reached for was the newspaper, and he read it through from page one to the end. Not only did he read the stories in the Literary Supplement, but he read all the articles on the politics of the day. Unlike his lessons which he could forget so easily, he remembered everything he read in the papers. He could name the ruling princes of the Balkan countries and all their prime ministers as well. And he knew by name all of the members of last three French cabinets, and what the latest speech in the German Reichstag was about.

The fifteen minutes passed quickly. When supper was ready, the newspapers were put aside, for the struggles with the lessons had to be taken up again as soon as the meal was over. And if there was still some time left before bedtime, Albert was made to practice on the piano again.

"You never know what good your music will be to you

when you're grown," his Aunt Sophie said, if he so much as made a small protest.

Something in him protested against the severe discipline of those years. Even the music he had loved became a chore for him. Instead of practicing the lesson his music teacher Eugen Münch had given him, he played whatever struck his fancy, making up tunes of his own.

"Albert Schweitzer is my thorn in the flesh," Eugen Münch once said of him.

He scolded the boy for what he called his "wooden playing."

"You have no feeling for music," he exclaimed.

No feeling for music! How could the teacher know? How could anyone know the way he felt deep inside him? These were things he could not bring himself to tell anyone. He remembered back to his first year at the village school, when he heard the older boys at their singing lesson. As young as he was then, he had been so moved by the sheer beauty of the two-part harmony that he had had to hold on to the wall to keep himself steady while the voices mingled. "In the mill by the stream below, there I was sitting quiet in thought. Beautiful forest, who planted you there?" The sound of the words stayed on in his mind. It had been the same when he heard for the first time brass instruments playing together. He thought he would surely faint from the sheer pleasure of listening. But these were things he could not talk about to anyone for fear of being misunderstood.

All week Albert found himself looking forward to Sunday in spite of the fact that the church services at Mulhouse made him more homesick than ever for Günsbach. He missed his father's gentle voice in the pulpit, and he missed also going to a church where those of different faiths could worship in harmony. But on Sunday afternoons he could go for walks with his uncle and aunt. Sedately he kept step with them, and in his thoughts he could roam far to the distant hills and over the long canal that flowed through the town. And every Sunday evening until ten o'clock he was free to read whatever he wanted.

Like a hungry child in a bakery shop he opened the pages of his book and read avidly. Aunt Sophie often looked up from her own book and frowned disapprovingly when she saw him turn the pages so quickly. She was quite sure no one could read that fast.

"That's no way to read a book, sniffing through the pages like that," she said. "A book should be read slowly so its style can be enjoyed. The way a book is written, that's the important thing."

Albert did not argue with her, for, after all, whether he had fifteen minutes more or less for reading depended entirely on his aunt's humor. But it seemed to him that if he could enjoy a book down to the last sentence, that should surely be proof enough that its style was good. And if there were long, boring passages he was tempted to skip, then it couldn't have been so well written.

Aunt Sophie was as strict with herself as she was with the boy in her care. She allowed herself three hours a day for reading, one hour before dinner and two hours after, and not one minute longer. Even then her fingers were busy with some knitting or crocheting while the book lay open on the table before her.

"Oh this man Daudet!" she would exclaim aloud once in a while. Or she would say, "Oh what a style this author has!"

The clicking of her needles slowed almost to a stop when she became absorbed, and if a book amused her very much, she laughed until tears came to her eyes. But no matter how interesting she found the book, or what part of a page she had reached when the hands of the clock pointed to half past ten, she promptly closed it, with a marker in place to show where she had left off. She went then to bed.

Albert longed to go on and finish his book to the end, even if it meant sitting up all night to do so. But he, too, had to put his book aside, and wait another week before he picked it up again.

At Christmas, Albert went back to Günsbach for the holidays. He was sure nothing could mar the happiness and freedom of this vacation in spite of the fact that this was the one time in the year when his father was as strict as Uncle Louis and Aunt Sophie, when it came to writing letters of thanks for the presents the children received. On a morning after Christmas he was sure to make the announcement:

"Today we'll get the letters written. You children like to accept presents, but when it comes to writing letters of thanks, you are too lazy. Set to work now, and don't let me see any sulky faces."

The children knew they had to obey. Albert sat at the desk in his father's study, rebelling as always in his heart at the task. It was enough to take away the pleasure of Christmas, to spend a whole day in a musty, book-lined room. When other boys were sliding on their sleds down the hill behind the church, Albert had to be writing to godparents, uncles and aunts and friends of his parents. There must not be a single mistake or blot. He could envy his sister Louise who managed to finish her letters in time to play, but often he sat till dark trying to think of how to thank each one in a different way, and tell about his other presents and wish each one a happy New Year.

He wouldn't mind it this time, he felt, for he would be willing to do anything for the joy of being home again. But when he arrived, he found that something had happened that worried his parents and spoiled the holidays for him as well.

His report card had such poor grades that there was doubt whether he would even be allowed to go to the school any longer. As a pastor's son, he had been given a free tuition, but this could not be kept up with such a record. His parents did not nag or scold, but Albert noticed that his mother's eyes were red from weeping, and there was a worried expression on his father's face. This troubled him more than if they had scolded. He knew he should have made more of an effort, that he might have spent the time over his lessons that had been given to daydreaming. But when he went back after the vacation was over, it was the same as before. This kept up, with the grades as low as ever and the teachers ready to throw up their hands in exasperation, until a new teacher, Dr. Wehmann, came to the school.

There was something about the way this teacher came to the classroom every day with the lesson so carefully prepared that impressed even a boy of eleven. Albert noticed how Dr. Wehmann seemed to know exactly how much of the subject he wanted to cover, and he managed to get through with it exactly as he had planned. On the proper day, and in the proper lesson hour, the exercise books he had taken up earlier were returned.

Albert admired the way this teacher worked, and began to use him for a model. He would start then to plan his own day with care, he decided. It became a kind of game with him to see how thoroughly he could prepare each lesson, and how many letters he could form in his copybook without making a blot or mistake. In three months' time he surprised his teachers and parents with grades high enough to place him near the top of the class. After that he carried this game of challenge on to the subjects for which he had no talent, such as mathematics and languages.

It wasn't easy, and often he had to study in his own way instead of the way the teachers wanted. Even in science and history, his favorite subjects, he had to reason things out for himself. In spite of his science textbook, he knew such things as shifting winds and clouds and thunder and the warm Gulf Stream could never be explained in so many words. There was a mysticism about nature, he felt, and every drop of rain and every snowflake with its unique pattern was something of a miracle. The more detailed the explanation about the way these things came about, the more mysterious they really were.

Gradually friendships were formed that were to mean a great deal to Albert, but they would have come much sooner, and he would have been spared the unhappiness of his first years at Mulhouse had he been less shy about showing his feelings, or if there had been someone in whom he could have confided.

When Wagner's opera *Tannhäuser* came to Mulhouse, Albert was allowed to go. It was the first time he had ever been inside a theater, and the music he heard that night affected him deeply. For several days afterward, he was so lost in the memory of it that he scarcely knew what else was going on around him, yet he could not bring himself to talk about it. His music teacher, Eugen Münch, little guessing the boy's thoughts, scolded him again for not knowing his lesson.

"Really you don't deserve to have such beautiful music given you to play," he said angrily, after Albert had finished playing a badly practiced sonata of Mozart.

As he spoke, he opened a volume of Mendelssohn's "Song Without Words in E Natural."

"You'll spoil this for me just as you've spoiled everything else," he went on with a resigned sigh. "If a boy has no feeling, I certainly can't give it to him."

Albert took the music without answering. It was something he had played often to himself, and no one knew better than he how much it had affected him.

"I'll show him," he said to himself, as he started back to his uncle's home. "I'll show him whether I have any feeling or not."

There was no daydreaming that week when he sat at the piano to practice. This was a challenge, just as his classroom lessons had become since the arrival of the new teacher. Not only did he go over and over the music assigned him, but he studied and experimented to learn the best fingering, and when he found the one that suited him he wrote it down above the notes.

At the next lesson, after the finger exercises and scales were finished, he started to play the "Song Without Words," fighting back as best he could that shyness he had of showing his true feelings. As he played on, he forgot the teacher standing over him, and lost himself completely in the music. When he came to the end, he waited for Eugen Münch to speak, but there was silence. He felt a hand grip his shoulder, gently pushing him up from the piano. Then Münch sat down to play, as one musician would play for another. It was another "Song Without Words" which Albert had never heard before. At that moment a deep friendship between teacher and pupil was started; a friendship which lasted until the death of the older man.

Albert was given a piece by Beethoven for his next lesson, and after that it was thought he was ready to start on Bach. As he practiced the constantly recurring rhythmical motives, he fell into the spirit of the music, which he was to describe much later as "the blessed peacefulness or lively joy as well as intense pain or pain sublimely borne." From this beginning there developed a lifelong interest in the great composer and his works.

He was promised lessons on the magnificent organ at St. Stephen, the Protestant Cathedral, where Münch played for the Sunday services. This was a dream he had long cherished, but he must wait until after his confirmation before he would be ready to begin.

He studied hard for the confirmation, as he had learned by now to do, but when the pastor who prepared the class began to question him, he was faced with that same difficulty in showing his true emotions. The pastor kept him back for a private talk, trying to find out what he felt about this holy time, but still Albert could not let the good man look so deeply into his heart. He hesitated over the answers he gave and turned some questions aside with no answer at all.

"He's going through his confirmation as one of the indifferent ones," the pastor said to Aunt Sophie afterward.

Aunt Sophie should surely have understood his reticence, for hadn't she always said that reserve was the essence of good breeding, and every kind of forwardness should be regarded as a serious fault?

The soul has a modesty that should be respected as much as modesty of the body, he thought. Years afterward he could look back on this day and still feel that no one should be forced to show more of his inner life than he felt it natural to show. Not even a mother had a right to tear the clothing from a soul, to force a way into the thoughts and heart of another.

On Palm Sunday, Albert marched with the other boys in procession from the vestry to the church, with Eugen Münch playing the organ he himself was so soon to commence practicing on. As he listened to the beautiful music from Handel's *Messiah*, "Lift up your heads, O ye gates!" he felt it was in wonderful harmony with his thoughts. And even while his uncle and aunt were feeling deeply concerned, and the pastor was looking upon him as indifferent, Albert was so moved by the beauty and solemnity of the occasion that he felt almost ill.

Soon after the confirmation, he was allowed to sit at the organ himself, running his fingers over the three keyboards and all the sixty-two stops. Later on he was able to take his teacher's place occasionally at the service and at last the time came when he played the accompaniment in a concert given by the church choir. He knew then the joy his Grandfather Schillinger must have felt when he sat at the organ, sending the rich, sonorous tones of Brahms's Requiem mingling with the resonant sounds of choir and orchestra.

The eight years which had seemed such an eternity when he had first come to Mulhouse, a lonely, homesick boy of nine, were now drawing to a close. Soon he would have to say good-by to the friends he had made and the teachers he had come to admire and respect. And the thought of leaving his Uncle Louis and Aunt Sophie filled him with the same sadness he had felt eight years before when he had left Günsbach to come here. Now that he was older, he could see that, with all their strict discipline, they had given him love and affection and a sense of security that boys away at school do not often find. He could look back at all the little things they had done to show their affection, though at the time he had scarcely noticed them.

He thought of a day in early spring during that first year when he was still homesick and longing for the freedom of his life at Günsbach. He had been sitting at the table, just after the four o'clock coffee hour, with his books before him, ready to go back to his homework. The day had been sunny and warm enough to melt the last ragged patches of snow that remained. Suddenly Aunt Sophie had looked up from her ironing and had seen him gazing longingly out of the window.

"Come," she had said, putting her iron back on the stove. "We'll go out for a little walk."

They had walked together in silence, on and on, over the canal where blocks of ice were floating, and then on up the southern slope of the hill where Albert could look out on the white peaks of the Vosges Mountains, which bordered the valley of home. He had expected at any moment to hear his aunt say they must turn around now and go back to the house, but she had kept on walking with him until it was too dark to go farther. Nothing was ever said about the walk, but from that day on there was a bond of understanding between them.

Now that he was older, he took his walks alone, and often his steps led to the slopes on the south side of the city, where he could see the mountains he loved. Sometimes he met an old man walking that way too, with his hat in one hand, his long hair blowing in the wind, and in his other hand he often carried a bunch of wild flowers he had gathered. They came in time to recognize each other and they would walk together through the fields and woods. The man was Adolph Ströber, the Alsatian poet, whose poems of the beauty of the country and the joys of friendship and family life were known to every schoolboy in Alsace.

Now that he was so soon to leave, Albert could count more happy memories than sad ones of the years he had spent here. And as much as he looked forward to his return to Günsbach, there was that same regret he always felt at leaving a familiar place.

The last day of examination was a solemn occasion. It was enough to fill any youth with awe to dress in a black frock coat and black trousers, and stand up in the long hall alone, while his classmates waited their turn, to answer questions put to him by the School Commissioner, who came down from Strasbourg for the occasion. Their teachers sat at a long table facing the boys, and looked on sternly or in anxiety, or with smiles of encouragement.

Albert had a black frock coat which had once belonged to a relative of his mother's, but he had no black trousers to match.

"I'll lend you mine," his Uncle Louis said.

Neither of them had given much thought to the difference in their sizes. His uncle was short and fat and Albert was tall and thin. When he tried on the trousers on the morning of the examination, they came scarcely to the tops of his high shoes. He tied a string to his suspenders to make them longer, but then there was a gap between the vest and the trousers. Well, it was too late now, he decided. He would have to wear them anyway.

His classmates, all properly dressed, took one look at him when he arrived at the school and began to laugh. Albert saw the humor in the situation and laughed with them. The boys turned him around so they could see how he looked from all sides, and there was so much laughter and hilarity that they couldn't change their expressions immediately, when they were told to enter the examination room. Even the teachers, sitting at the table, smiled when they saw Albert come in, but the School Commissioner gave him a stern frown. What kind of clowning was this meant to be, his expression plainly said. He singled out the one he thought to be the cause of such misbehavior and began to examine him personally. Question after question was asked. The principal, who once had been worried enough over Albert's low grades during that first year, now gave him looks of encouragement. But the Commissioner shook his head all the more when an answer was wrong.

"How did they beach the ships, as described by Homer?" he asked.

The tales of Homer were filled with adventure enough to hold the attention of any boy, but it had never seemed important to Albert, reading them, to know just how ships were beached at that time. He had never been interested in memorizing the names of all the ancestors and relations of the gods and heroes. The other boys in the class knew little more than Albert did, and a lecture was delivered by the disapproving Commissioner.

Albert waited in suspense for the next subject. Would it be mathematics, the one he was weakest in, he wondered. If so, he would surely fail. But the Commissioner was not too good at that himself, so he began on his own favorite subject, history. These were the questions Albert could answer best. He could see the man's anger slowly melt until finally, instead of asking questions, he began to discuss certain things that happened in the past, as one would with an equal. He talked about the difference between the colonizing effects of the Greeks and those of the Romans, apparently forgetting entirely that he was holding an examination.

Albert's grades were not among the highest in the class, but on his certificate there were words of praise for his history examination, in the Commissioner's own handwriting.

When the examinations were over, Albert said good-by to his uncle and aunt, and never had they been more dear to him than at that moment. He could wonder now how the last eight years had passed so quickly. He was a boy of nine when he had first come, so reluctantly, to Mulhouse, and now he was returning home, a youth of seventeen, robust and tall for his age.

The Schweitzer family had moved from the old manse, with its damp, dark walls, to another set in a sunny garden. Albert's father had set out young trees there, propping up the trunks with stakes to make them grow straighter. And oleander bushes bloomed in wooden tubs beside the doorstep.

The past years had brought little change to Albert's parents. His father's beard was black with no trace of gray. And his mother was still slender and looked as young as on the day he had left. But his brother Paul, a chubby, round-faced child then, was now almost as tall as he was. And his sisters had become young ladies. The two oldest wore their hair pinned up as grownups did, and even Adele, the youngest, dressed in a

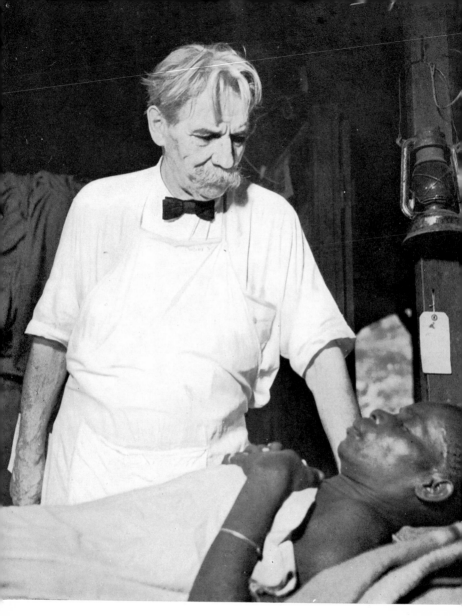

Dr. Schweitzer visits a post-operative patient

long skirt and a shirtwaist with leg-of-mutton sleeves, like the ones her older sisters wore.

A photographer came to take a picture of the whole family soon after Albert's return. They gathered in the garden beside the house, and even the dog lay curled at his master's feet, to be included. Albert and Paul brought out their bicycles and stood beside them proudly while the others sat in chairs and on the steps between them.

A bicycle was something unusual in Günsbach then. It had been only ten years since the first one was seen coming through the village. Albert had been a child in his first year at school then, and he had gone with the other children during recess time to stare at this strange contraption. And how they had all laughed to see the rider wearing knickers like their own, instead of long trousers such as grownups wore.

Some of the villagers frowned at the sight of the pastor's sons riding bicycles. It wasn't seemly, they said. But Pastor Schweitzer made no objection. Albert had earned the money himself for his, by tutoring backward pupils during his last years at the Mulhouse school. And his father understood what it meant to a boy to be able to ride far out along country lanes, taking in mile after mile of meadows and forest.

Albert felt at times that he must surely be the most fortunate person in all the world. He had a happy home. There was affection and security and abounding good health. His father, who had been ill often in the old manse, had completely recovered since moving to their new home, and a small legacy left to his mother had removed the most pressing financial worries. Albert himself, who had been such a weak, sickly baby, had strength and energy enough to accomplish anything he set his mind to do. He made his plans to go to the University of Strasbourg that fall. And after that, there was the whole world ahead of him.

He could not think of these things, however, without thinking also of those who were not so fortunate, and he was troubled. Why should his life be better than another's? What right had he to accept this happiness as his due, when somewhere there were others suffering sorrow or pain? Surely there was something he could do to help, but what could it be?

Chapter V

Grow into your ideals so that life can never rob you of them. If all of us could become what we were at fourteen, what a different place this world would be.

Memoirs of Childhood and Youth

THERE WAS A SPIRIT of freedom about the University of Strasbourg at the close of the last century. The professors were for the most part young, and they had no patience with the old, outmoded methods of other universities, constantly concerned as they were with examinations taken from dull textbooks. There was something contagious about the enthusiasm of these younger professors in their classroom lectures, and professors and students all worked together to make it an ideal university.

Before enrolling for his classes at Strasbourg, Albert Schweitzer spent a month in Paris visiting an uncle who lived there. While he was there he was able to take lessons from Charles Widor, one of the most famous organists of his day. It was too short a time to learn much more than how much he needed to study to improve his technique, in order to acquire that perfect plasticity he wanted in his playing.

It was at the end of October in 1893 when he arrived at Strasbourg. There were not enough hours in the day for all the things he wanted to do. He chose courses in theology, for he wanted to preach, as his father did. And he studied philosophy, and also the technique of music. Even this was not enough. He wanted to know how to read the Old Testament in the original, so he took up the study of Hebrew. And he found time to study and play on the organ at St. William's Church not far from the University, where Ernest Münch, a brother of his teacher at Mulhouse, was organist.

Like his brother, Ernest Münch was also especially interested in Bach, and he started a series of Bach concerts there with choir and orchestra and organ. During the rehearsals, Albert played the accompaniment for the cantatas and the Passion music. Later, when the organist, Eugen Münch, was unable to come up from Mulhouse, Albert was allowed to play at the actual performance.

When he was nineteen, Albert had to take his year of military training, as the sexton Jaegle had predicted. He went through the drills and marches with other boys his age, but he had the strength of a young giant and never knew what it was to feel tired. Whenever he could find the time, he took his regular place in the classrooms. And when his company went on maneuvers, there was a Greek testament in his knapsack, which he studied at night and during the periods of rest, for there was a scholarship he hoped to win, to help pay his way through the University.

He could look back with some amusement now on those first heartbreaking years at Mulhouse, when he whiled away his time in idle daydreams. And when he had come out of those dreams and begun to study in earnest, what a nuisance he must have been. He could call them now his salad years, when he had annoyed his elders by insisting upon discussing with them the questions of the day, and arguing with them to clarify his own ideas. But they were not wasted years. That curiosity he had shown as a child, when he had wondered what the parents of Jesus did with the gifts the Wise Men brought, and that tireless searching for the meaning of things, now took him deeper into his studies. He was not satisfied with what he read in books, or with what the professors said in the classrooms.

He must find out for himself, and reason things out in his own way. Nor had he lost his dreams entirely, but the dreams now had meaning and led him on in his search for truth. He could sit thinking and dreaming of the many miracles of life that were everywhere around him, a blade of grass, flower petals opening, floating clouds, waving fields of ripened grain. And he thought of how the lowliest, smallest creature had the will to live, even as he had.

One morning during Whitsuntide, when he had gone home to Günsbach for the holidays, he woke up thinking again of how much he had to be thankful for. From his window he could hear the songs of the birds and the peaceful sounds of a village just awakening. It was good to be back home again with his gentle, understanding parents and his sisters and brother. It was also good to be able to go to the University. He loved the room he had there at the College of St. Thomas, looking out on the quiet, walled-in garden with its large shade trees. His studies were more like a game to him now, planning and preparing each one in the way he did. He thought of the pleasant evenings, too, with Ernest Münch, the organist, going over the scores of the Bach cantatas and talking together of the way they were meant to be performed.

Again the question came to him when such thoughts as these ran through his head. Had he a right to this happiness? He felt now the same as he had when he was a child and had learned that George Nitschelm could not have nourishing broth such as he had for his supper. It was like a small cloud hovering on the horizon. He might turn away and forget it for a time, but it was still there, just the same, slowly growing and slowly coming closer. At last he knew that he could ignore it no longer. As long as there were people in the world suffering from pain and want, it was not enough that he should accept his own happiness and perfect health without a thought for others. He had a strength that gave him power to work and study day and night without ever knowing what it was to feel tired. Now he must give this strength to help others. He had been spared pain. Now he must try in some way to ease the pain of others. He must carry his own share of the misery of the world, instead of turning his back upon it and living for himself alone. The meaning of words in the Bible, hidden from him until then, became clear. "Whosoever would save his life shall lose it, and whosoever shall lose his life for My sake, shall save it."

On that June morning, when the sun came slanting through the windows of his room at the manse, Albert Schweitzer made a resolution that became the turning point of his life. He was twenty-one then. He would spend the next nine years, until he was thirty, doing the things he wanted to do, such as keeping on with his studies in science and music, and working as a pastor, as his father did. After that, he would give up these things and devote the rest of his life to serving mankind in some more direct way. Just what that way would be and how he would go about it, he was not sure. But now that he had made his decision, he had a feeling of inward peace.

Seldom in one lifetime have there been such crowded years, with so much accomplished, as those that followed. With his first examination in theology, Albert Schweitzer won the scholarship which allowed him to go on with his studies. He spent a winter in Paris, a summer in Berlin, then he was back at the University of Strasbourg to work for his doctor's degree in both philosophy and theology. His grades were never among the highest in any of his classes, but he had the kind of inquiring mind that sent him delving into a subject, searching out the answers for himself, instead of accepting some dogmatic statement in a book. When he came upon some mention about a theory of a certain philosopher who lived long ago, or something about the writings of an obscure, forgotten person, he was not satisfied until he went back and read the original, to form his own opinion. He felt he must read all the chief works of ancient and modern philosophy.

One bit of information led to another, and his curiosity took him on in search of still more. The subject of the Last Supper was given to all the students of theology to write about. Albert went back to the Greek Testament, and to every book he could find about the Gospels and every book about the life of Jesus. He was not satisfied with that, but he also studied the customs and ways of the people living at the time that Jesus lived. He began to interpret certain passages in his own way, even though it varied from the accepted beliefs of the time.

He was doing the work of three men in those years, with the three careers he followed. When he had his degree, he was made Principal of the Theological College where he had attended as a student. He was given new living quarters there, but he still kept as a study the old room which he loved. From that room he could look out on the gentle river Ill, where red-cheeked children played at tag among the poplars on the banks or romped along the grassy slopes. A short distance away from the College, on the other side of the river, the steep roof of the little Church of St. Nicholas could be seen, with its three stories of dormer windows. It was the church where Albert Schillinger, the uncle for whom he was named, had been pastor thirty years before. Now he, too, was one of the pastors there. It was a pleasant walk from the College to the church, and on along the riverbank to the University, where he gave lectures in philosophy. And not far from the University, there was the Church of St. William, where he played the organ for the Bach concerts.

Life was pleasant for him in those days, serene, yet full and busy with the things he liked best to do. He still had the health and the strength and energy of his student days, and many a night the lamps were burning in the student room that had become his study, long after all the other rooms of the city

71

were dark. He prepared his lectures and his sermons, and there were the duties as Principal of the College. Still he found time to add another career, that of writing.

He had his grandfather's love for the organ, and the same curiosity about how they were made. Like his grandfather, he often went far out of his way to see a new one being built, and to learn how the different tones were produced. This led to an essay, which he called "The Art of Organ Building and Organ Playing in Germany and France."

It was Charles Widor, the organist under whom he had studied in Paris, who encouraged him in this. They had become close friends, and often, on his visits to Paris, the two would sit long hours at a little restaurant near Widor's studio and talk of Bach and the way his music should be played. This led to discussions of old organs, the kind the composer himself had played and written his music for. The modern organs were more elaborate and had been built for size, they agreed, but Bach had written for the kind with keys that moved slowly and needed to be firmly pressed. The new organs had not been built with love and care as the older ones had, and much was lost when Bach was played with huge orchestras and massed choirs.

The essay about organs was followed by a book called *Bach, the Musician Poet*. And there were plans for still another one as a result of the research into the life of Jesus. In the corners against the walls, and between the pieces of furniture in Albert Schweitzer's study, there were piles of all the books written about Jesus that he had been able to find in libraries and bookstores. Each pile of books was for a separate chapter of the book he planned to write, and he wanted none disturbed until that chapter was finished. Friends who came to visit had to step carefully from one cleared space to another, between books marked *early fictitious lives, liberal lives, imaginative lives, skeptical lives,* down to the latest nineteenth-century books on Jesus.

In the midst of this busy life, there kept coming back to his mind, like a recurring melody in a symphony, the memory of his vow made when he was twenty-one. Yes, at thirty he would give up these things and devote the rest of his life to serving his fellow men. It had not occurred to him that he would carry on this work anywhere but in Alsace, close to his own home. There were children in Strasbourg, destitute and neglected, who needed help. And there were tramps, wandering homeless from place to place, and men discharged from prisons who needed encouragement to guide them on the way to a new life.

While he was still a student, Albert Schweitzer had made a start in this work. With other students he had joined an organization doing social service work. They had gone about asking for contributions from the wealthy, who could afford to give. This was torture at first for the shy, sensitive youth, but it was worth any embarrassment he had felt when he visited the families of the poor and saw their need.

He might have considered that he was serving mankind enough in his work as pastor. His sermons were given with the same simplicity and sincerity that he had admired in his father's. And when he gave instruction to the young people for their confirmation, he remembered his own school days at Mulhouse, and he knew that more went on in the hearts of boys and girls than they showed on the surface. They felt his sympathy and understanding and had confidence in him, knowing they could come to him with whatever problems they might have.

This was still not what he had had in mind when at twenty-one he had made his vow on that morning in June. He was approaching thirty now and the decision of just what kind of work he would do had still not been made. He felt like a man who saw a light shining far away through semidarkness, and he went on groping toward it, knowing that he would find there the thing that he was searching for.

It was not until the fall of the year, a few months before his thirtieth birthday, that he found this light and knew what he would do. Someone had placed a little green-covered pamphlet on his writing table, and he came across it there among his books and papers. It was a pamphlet distributed by the Paris Missionary Society every month, the kind he had often seen and read. Late in the evening he paused briefly in his work and started to leaf through the pages, when his eye fell by chance on the title of an article, "The Needs of the Congo Mission."

Memories came to him of the articles written for this same publication by the missionary Casalis, which his father had read long ago during his Sunday afternoon services at Günsbach. This article told of the same need for workers in Africa that Casalis had written of a generation ago. The author, an Alsatian, described the Gabon, that remotest of regions in the French Colony near the African Equator, and he made an appeal for those who would offer themselves for this urgent work.

"Men and women who can reply simply to the Master's call, 'Lord I am coming,' these are the people whom the church needs."

Albert Schweitzer read on to the last sentence. Then he quietly put the pamphlet aside and went on with the work before him. His search was over now. His decision was made. It was as if this were something he had known all along, something beyond words or thoughts, but felt deep in his heart.

For the next few months he went on as if nothing had happened. He preached in the little Church of St. Nicholas and gave instruction for confirmation. He lectured at the University and worked on his research into the life of Jesus. And often when there was an hour to spare in the day or night, he would go quietly to St. William's Church and play on the

organ, losing himself in the music of Bach and other com-
posers he admired.

There was a portrait painted of him at that time by the young
artist, Ada von Erlach. She was frail and weak from a recent
operation, and Albert hoped, that, with this work to keep her
interested, she would begin to feel well again. The portrait was
finished on the fourteenth of January, his thirtieth birthday.
The likeness had been easy enough to catch on canvas, with
the dark hair, the bristling mustache, the broad shoulders, and
eyes that were keen and penetrating, yet had something of the
dreamer as well. But Ada von Erlach, artist though she was,
aware of every curve and every shadow that showed the slightest hint of the expression in a face, little dreamed the thoughts
that went on in the mind of Albert Schweitzer then. He had
spoken to no one about his plans. But now, from that day on,
his old life was at an end, and a new life was beginning.

Chapter VI

No one who is always striving to refine his character can ever be robbed of his idealism, for he experiences in himself the power of the ideas of the good and the true.

Memoirs of Childhood and Youth

ON A DAMP FOGGY DAY near the end of October of that same year, the young medical students in the anatomy class saw a man of thirty come into the room and take his place as a freshman among them. He was tall and strongly built, with dark, unruly hair and the kind of heavy, bristling mustache popular with the men of the time. His hazel eyes had a way of twinkling with ready laughter and friendship, yet there was something also in their expression which set him apart from others in the room.

Some of the students might have recognized him as the professor who lectured on philosophy at the University. Others may have heard his sermons at the Church of St. Nicholas beside the river Ill, or they might have known him as the Principal of the Theological College. And those who loved music had heard him play the organ at the Bach concerts at St. William's Church near by.

But what was he doing here, they wondered. Why would he be starting as a freshman in this class on anatomy? They saw him again in the other classes, in physiology, chemistry, physics, zoology and botany, listening to the lectures and taking notes as they were doing. But why?

The students were not the only ones who asked the question. The dean of the medical school himself, the professors in the

Philosophy Department and all of Albert Schweitzer's other friends were asking the same question. Why should a man who already had a doctor's degree in theology and another in philosophy, whose book, *Bach, the Musician Poet*, just published in French, was so popular there was now a demand for it in German, too, and whose essay on organs had been widely read, be coming here now as a freshman to begin the long, hard course in medicine?

It had not been an easy decision for Albert Schweitzer to make. He could look with impatience upon the stretch of years ahead, when he must prepare for the work he had undertaken. But he had thought his reasons for it would be understood. From Paris, where he had gone that summer, he had written to relatives and a few close friends, telling of his plan to begin the study of medicine so that he could give the help most needed to the people of Africa.

"But why should a man of your ability, and with a future of such promise, throw it all away to go off to the jungles of Africa?" they exclaimed.

Oh yes, they said, they understood people were suffering there from famine and disease and pain. And help was needed more there, perhaps, than in any other place in the world.

"But why should you be the one to go? Why not leave such work as that to others, who don't have so much to sacrifice?"

"Couldn't you accomplish much more by staying here and giving lectures to raise money for them?" one asked.

Even the musician Widor, who loved him as if he had been his own son, compared him to a general wanting to go into the firing line himself. And he begged him to think it over carefully before coming to such a decision. Others, not so kind, began to hint at some secret motive, such as disappointment because fame had not come as quickly as he might have wanted, though they must have realized this could not be true. He had already made a name for himself with his concerts and lectures and with his writings. There were even those who wondered if some unhappy love affair had been the cause of his decision. How strange it was, young Schweitzer thought, that they could guess at every reason but the right one.

To him this was nothing out of the ordinary that he had chosen to do. He hadn't thought of sacrifice or heroism. He simply recognized it as a duty which, he told himself, should be done with quiet enthusiasm. It was in this same way that Simon and Andrew had responded when Jesus, walking by the Sea of Galilee, had called to them.

And straightway they forsook their nets and
followed him.

Far from looking upon this as a sacrifice, he could feel he was unusually fortunate. He had health, sound nerves, energy, practical common sense, toughness, prudence, and very few wants, everything needed for just such work as he had chosen. And he was free to go where he was needed. He thought of the many others who must have had this same impulse to follow the kind of life he had chosen, but who had to give it up because of ill health or some claim of others dependent upon them.

He tried to explain these things, in spite of his normal reserve about showing his inmost feelings. It seemed to him that these people were trying to tear open all the doors and shutters of his inner being. It was as if they were digging fists into his heart. The ones he resented least were those who teased affectionately, calling him a bright young man but a little touched in the head.

"Oh well, these things have to be," he said to himself.

There was no use showing anger. Why should anyone who sets about to do a thing worth while expect others to roll stones out of the way for him, he reasoned. Even if a few more stones were rolled in the way, it was best to accept it calmly. These very obstacles could give him a strength needed to conquer.

With true Alsatian stubbornness he went on, for he knew the way he was going and nothing could turn him aside. If at times he looked at the long years of work and preparation ahead and felt discouraged and impatient, he thought of Hannibal and Hamilcar who had prepared for their march on Rome by their slow and tedious conquest of Spain.

More than ever he had to plan his days and nights so there would be time for all he had to do. For the first time he began to know what it was to feel tired. There was a constant fight now against weariness. In his student days, his studies had come to him naturally, for he came from a family of musicians and pastors and had grown up in that atmosphere. But in medicine he found himself in a different world, one where he must learn to adjust himself. In philosophy and in history, the subjects that had been easiest for him, there could be endless arguments over whether certain statements were true or false, and often the exact answer is never known. But in chemistry and physics, every statement made must be proved. As always, when a thing seemed difficult, he made of it a kind of challenge, and it became a game for him of searching for the answer.

Like Simon and Andrew, and James and John who left the ship where they had been mending nets when Jesus called, Albert Schweitzer left his old familiar life to follow the new. He resigned his post as Principal of the Theological College, and left the place where he had lived since his student days. On a rainy Mardi Gras, the students helped him move into four attic rooms in the home of the president of the Lutheran Church of Alsace. The lamplight shone from these windows sometimes the whole night through. And the next morning Albert Schweitzer set out to attend his classes in medicine and to give his lectures in philosophy at the University, having had scarcely any sleep the night before. On these days, when the classes were over, he found himself stopping off at the Church of St. William to chat with Ernest Münch, the organist, and to play on the organ himself. After an hour of Bach, he felt calm and rested through the healing powers of this great musician's work.

At his new living quarters he came and went as if he were a part of the family. Sometimes, when there was an hour to spare out of a busy day, he sat down at the piano to play for the aged Countess von Erlach, who lived there with her three daughters and her son-in-law. She loved music devotedly, and now that she was old and feeble and could not move about easily, she missed more than anything else the concerts she had once attended. She loved to talk of the old days, of things that had happened long ago and the people she had known when she lived in the household of Emperor Frederick's sister, the Grand Duchess Louise of Baden.

Once young Schweitzer led her to the window of her room, for she was not able to walk alone, where they could look out and see the first airplane that ever flew over Strasbourg. They marveled at the way it flew low past the house, then swooped up in the skies again, until it disappeared from sight.

"What a strange life I've led," the old Countess said. "I've discussed past participles with Alexander von Humboldt in my youth, and now I am a witness to man's conquest of the air."

She liked to talk of her uncle who had been an officer in the Dutch colonial service. In all the years he had spent in the tropics, she said, he had not once taken a fever.

"It was because he always wore his helmet," she went on. "And when you go to Africa, you must promise never to go out of doors bareheaded during the day, even after the sun has set."

There had been a financial struggle in the beginning of the medical course, with the source of most of his income gone after he resigned his post as Principal of the Theological College. But the reputation of Albert Schweitzer grew, both as a musician and a writer. It was almost as if temptations were put before him to try to lure him away from the kind of life he had planned for himself. In Paris he, with six other musicians, had formed a Bach Society, and now he was asked to give concerts not only in Paris, but in other parts of France, in Germany, and in Spain, where he played before the King and Queen at Madrid. His latest book, *The Quest of the Historical Jesus*, was published in English as well as French and German. It was widely read, and praised by Catholics and Protestants alike. And the German edition of his book on Bach was well received.

He had the gift of friendship. Those who met him, and even those who knew him only by his writings, felt instinctively his sincerity and the greatness of his spirit. Many new friends were added to the old, to whom he was always to remain loyal. There was Cosima Wagner, the widow of the composer, and their two sons, Romain Rolland, the writer, Luis Milet, and other writers and musicians of the time.

Carmen Sylva, the Queen of Roumania, wrote to praise him for making her beloved Bach still dearer to her, and she invited him to spend his holidays at the palace, where he would have nothing more to do than play the organ an hour or so a day for her. But there was no time in his busy schedule for holidays.

There was one other among the new friends, Helene Bresslau, the pretty young daughter of one of the professors of history at the University of Strasbourg. She had been a student there herself, and she understood and sympathized with Albert Schweitzer's decision.

The week before Christmas of 1911, almost seven years after Albert Schweitzer's thirtieth birthday, he took his last examination. As he walked out in the early winter darkness, he scarcely knew whether this was real or whether he was dreaming that the long preparation was over and the goal in sight. The surgeon teacher who had examined him walked beside him.

"It's only that you have such excellent health that you've been able to get through all this." The surgeon repeated the words several times, and his voice seemed to come from far away.

The year that followed was one of mingled emotions. He was almost ready to take up his new life, but there was the final break to be made with the old. He gave up the lecturing at the University and left his post as pastor at the Church of St. Nicholas. He felt a touch of sadness at the very thought of never teaching and never preaching any more. He went to Paris to take up work in the hospital and to study more about tropical medicine, and it was just as well to make the break from Strasbourg then, for he knew he would feel pain and regret every time he passed the little church beside the river Ill, or looked up at the windows of that second lecture room to the east of the entrance of the great university building.

Helene Bresslau, in the meantime, was making preparations also for this new life, for they were to be married the following June, when the doctor returned to Strasbourg. She had been a great help in the work of getting together his manuscripts and correcting proof. Now she began training to become a nurse in order to help with the work in Africa.

Theirs was a busy honeymoon, for there were so many things to do, and the time was drawing near when they must leave. They spent the remaining months at Günsbach in the manse with Albert's parents.

There were many journeys made from there, to buy supplies and give last concerts. But it was always good to return to the quiet, peaceful village of his childhood, to be with his family and to see again the friends he had grown up with.

In less than a year enough money had been raised through the concerts and lectures, and through the generosity of friends, to pay for building and maintaining a hospital in the jungles of Africa, enough to keep it going for two years. The congregation of his little Church of St. Nicholas contributed a share, and also the doctor's fellow professors at the University.

The exasperating chores of shopping for days on end and ordering from catalogues were at last at an end. Seventy packing cases were filled and their covers screwed down tightly. There were detailed lists of what each one contained, drugs, bandages and all the supplies needed to start a hospital from the beginning. And two steamer tickets were bought for Port Gentil, French Equatorial Africa.

Chapter VII

No man is ever completely and permanently a stranger to his fellow man. Man belongs to man. Man has claims on man.

Memoirs of Childhood and Youth

THE CHURCH BELLS RANG in the village of Günsbach for the afternoon services on Good Friday of 1913. It had been thirty-two years since the sound of them had caused a small boy to throw down his slingshot and scatter the birds in the orchard, to protect them from the stones of his companion. Now Albert Schweitzer, a man of forty, heard them again as he waited with his wife at the railway station for the train to start them on their journey into the unknown.

The years between had been a long and continuous preparation for the new life he was facing, though he may not have been aware of it in the beginning. When the last sound of the bells was still echoing through the valley, the little local train could be heard giving its long sharp blast, as it rounded the bend through the woods. There were kisses and handshakes and last-minute good-bys to the relatives and friends who had come to see them off. The doctor and his wife stood on the rear platform of the train when it started on its way again, for one last look toward their friends and the village, fast receding. The spire of the church steeple rose high above the tall trees on one side, and on the other there were the brown and purple waves of the Vosges Mountains, with the neat, green valley below.

This was the land Albert Schweitzer had always known and loved, a land of old castles high on a hillside, of green wheat-fields and orderly vineyards planted in straight, even rows. It was a smiling land, a land of rhythmically changing seasons, of fresh sweet violets and yellow broom grass in the spring, of bright flames of poppies and blue cornflowers in summer, autumn grapes and golden fields of grain, then the dry husks of winter, with seeds bursting through the pods. And spring again with the first crocus pushing through the cool earth.

There was that same touch of sadness which he always felt when he turned away from a familiar and well-loved scene. In Strasbourg he said good-by again to old friends there. And in Paris he heard Charles Widor play for the Easter services on the dear old organ of the Church of San Suplice. It was a fitting memory for Albert Schweitzer to take away with him, feeling as he did that from that day on there would be no more music in his life. It was better to renounce music entirely, he decided, and to let his fingers grow stiff from disuse of the keys. That way would make it easier for him.

The whole Easter day was like a glorious dream to be remembered long after. The sun shone brightly, and there seemed to be a gaiety about the people, dressed as they were in their holiday attire. Sounds of church bells came floating from a distance on the warm spring breeze. To the couple sitting in the train that afternoon, speeding on their way to the coast, it was like a joyous message to send them on their way. Yet at the same time there was a strange foreboding. There were hints of a coming war. The doctor had hoped and worked to bring about a better understanding between France and Germany, the two countries that laid claim to Alsace. He felt that neither side actually wanted war, and citizens of both were doing all they could to prevent it. But there were certain things that kept people on edge—like Russia speeding the building of strategic railways through Poland, and gold being withdrawn from circulation in both France and Germany, with paper money issued to take its place.

The little cargo steamer that sailed between Europe and West Africa was of shallow build, to allow it to go some distance up the Congo River. It swayed and dipped with each movement of the waves, backward and forward and sideways, like a great rocking horse that had lost its balance.

"Oh, that Bay of Biscay," one of the fellow passengers said with a sigh.

"How I wish it were all behind us," another added.

Albert and Helene Schweitzer listened quietly, feeling in their inexperience like poor, untraveled home birds finding themselves with a migratory flock. The other passengers were army officers, doctors, civil service officials and a few women returning from a vacation in their homeland to join their husbands stationed in Africa. They were all experienced travelers, and spoke so knowingly of high waves and storms at sea that tossed a boat as if it were a child's toy. There was something so determined and energetic about them, and they went on talking together, paying little attention to the two newcomers on their first voyage out. There came to Albert Schweitzer's mind the memory of the fowls his mother used to buy from the Italian poultry dealers every summer to add to her flock. He thought of how they would walk about for several days, shy and humble, among the older, knowing ones. But after the second day at sea he shared the experience of a storm as violent as any the most seasoned voyager had told about.

It came in the night with such force that the trunks in the cabin slid from one wall to the other with each lunge of the ship, and the hat cases went dashing after like rough children at play. The doctor tried to catch them, but after almost crushing his leg in the effort, he gave it up and went back to his berth, where he lay counting the seconds that passed between a lunge of the ship and the tumbling of the trunks. There were sounds from other cabins too, of wildly tossing objects, and the dishes in the galley rattled and crashed.

Without a sign of easing, the storm kept up for three nights and days. After the first night, the steward made fast the trunks and boxes so they no longer careened about the cabin floor. But in the galley the cooks dared not light a fire, and all the meals were served cold.

After the third day, when the storm had abated, the passengers began to emerge from their cabins. They felt drawn closer together after the experience shared, and there were friendly talks as they stood on deck looking out on the distant coast where a snow-capped mountain lost itself in the clouds. The sea was as blue as the sky, and white-foamed waves lapped gently at the sides of the boat. Now and then a flying fish leaped up from the water like a soaring bluebird, then dropped in again with a flash.

They reached the port of Dakar, and there Albert and Helene Schweitzer put on their helmets and went ashore, touching foot on African soil for the first time. Loungers in front of the hotels or at the sidewalk cafés looked on listlessly, but this was a solemn occasion for the couple they saw walking up the hilly streets. There were bird songs they had never heard before, and they saw tall trees and flowery shrubs with names they had yet to learn. They saw the misery of Africa as well as its beauty on that day. There were men in filthy rags that scarcely covered them, half-starved dogs that wandered aimlessly about and horses like skeletons, with their sides scraped raw and the sores daubed with Prussian blue.

They came upon a cart piled high with wood, stuck in a deep rut. Two Negroes, perched on the high seat, were trying to make their horse move on by shouts and heavy blows with a stick. The doctor was moved with that immense pity he felt for any suffering creature. When he was a child at Colmar and had seen the old limping horse beaten and tugged toward the slaughterhouse, he could do nothing but turn away, haunted ever after by the sight. But now there was something he could do.

"That's no way to get your cart out of the rut," he called to the men.

He had them get down off the seat and help, as he pushed with all his strength at the back. At last the wheel was free and the cart could move on.

"If you don't like to see animals mistreated, don't come to this country," an army officer, who had looked on from a distance, said when they returned to the boat.

They moved on down the coast of Africa, keeping almost always within sight of land. The Pepper Coast, the Ivory Coast, the Gold Coast, the Slave Coast. Magnificent green forests came right down to the water's edge, where waves broke upon the sands, sending up great clouds of spray. Grand Bassam and Cotonou. Now, one by one, at each port of call, there were hearty farewells as some passenger, a stranger such a short while ago, took his leave.

"Good health to you! Good health!"

The words were spoken with a smile, but they had a serious meaning here in the steamy tropics.

"Good health to you!"

Albert Schweitzer stood on deck and said good-by to the military doctor whom he had come to know. He had spent many hours during the voyage with this doctor, learning all he could about tropical illnesses and how they could be cured. Now he saw the doctor step into the wooden box to be lowered by a swinging crane into a little boat that danced up and down upon the waves below.

What kind of life, out there beyond the green forest, was waiting, he wondered, for these people to whom he had said good-by? How would they look when they came back after the years they must spend here? And would some of them come back at all?

Libreville and Cape Lopez. Now Albert and Helene Schweitzer, with trunks and bags and seventy cases of supplies, left the boat.

"Good health to you!" their fellow passengers still on board called out to them.

There were two hundred miles more to go before they reached their destination. The stern-paddled river boat *Alembe* took them on as passengers early on an April morning, and they began their way up the river Ogowe.

They had seen pictures of tropical jungles, with giant trees and brightly flowered creepers tangled around their trunks and in their branches. But with the scene now before their eyes, it was like some fantastic painting drawn from the artist's imagination and coming suddenly to life.

The doctor found his thoughts reaching back to the familiar landscape of Alsace. The Ogowe was not a river like the Rhine. It was a whole system of rivers, branching out and twisting back together again, making islands and lakes in between. And each branch was as big as the Rhine itself. How could the black pilot ever know which course to take, he wondered. But the pilot steered on without a map, guiding the boat with a sure hand from main stream to narrow channel, through a lake, then back to the main stream again.

The gray buttressed trees growing at the water's edge took on folds like a woman's gray silk skirt, giving them the appearance of being in motion. Now and then a dead tree rose high above the others, with branches like graceful arms held in rigid poses. The islands were covered with papyrus growing as tall as a man, their feathery leaves waving in the wind so that the smaller islands seemed to be floating gently down the stream. A snow-white heron rose silently and heavily to perch on a higher tree. Kingfishers skimmed over the water, and a pair of ospreys circled high overhead. Then, from the branch of a palm, two monkey tails could be seen swinging to and fro. Two pairs of bright monkey eyes looked down upon the boat in curiosity. Yes, this was truly Africa.

Now and then they passed a native village where half-naked, laughing children came out of straw-thatched mud huts to stare at them. Sometimes they came upon a village that was completely deserted, where huts were crumbling to ruins and no sign of life could be seen anywhere.

"Fifteen years ago, when I first came out here, this was a flourishing village," a trader standing beside Dr. Schweitzer remarked.

"And why isn't it so any longer?" the doctor asked.

The trader shrugged his shoulders and said one word. "Alcohol."

This, too, was Africa. Would any amount of help given these people ever outweigh the evils brought also by the white man, Albert Schweitzer wondered.

The boat stopped at a village to take on wood, and a line of carriers came walking up the gangplank, each with a load of logs balanced on his head.

"Put a one," a man called out as in a chant for each ten logs counted, while another made a mark on a piece of paper. "Put a one. Put a one." And when the hundredth log was counted, he changed his call to, "Put a cross."

Darkness came suddenly with the setting of the sun, and it was as though it brought with it the shadow of all the misery of this land. Help was needed badly here, the doctor could clearly see with every village he passed. And it must be brought by men who would not ever let themselves be discouraged.

The forest rose like an immense black wall along the river-bank, with the boat approaching close enough at times to seem to graze its sides. The stars, small and far away in the misty tropical night, seemed to have veered from their accustomed places, and there were new ones in the south, never seen in the Alsatian sky. Far in the distance there was a flash of heat light-ning. The boat dropped anchor in a quiet bay when there was no longer light enough to steer by. Then at the first gray light of dawn it started on its way again. By midmorning the slopes of Lambaréné could be seen.

There was a long blast of the siren which brought the traders and merchants of Lambaréné to the landing for the cargo they were expecting. The boat had scarcely landed, when a long narrow canoe came shooting around its sides so fast a white man at the stern had just time to throw himself backward to keep from hitting the boat's cable. But the black boys rowing kept up the merry song they had been singing to the rhythm of the paddle strokes. These were the boys of the mission school with their teacher, racing a group of older boys of the mission, who came paddling up later. Because the younger boys had won, they were allowed to take the doctor and his wife in their canoe to the mission site, an hour's journey farther upstream. And the older boys followed with the luggage.

The spirit of the race was still on, and the boys standing at the oars tried to pass all the canoes and even the river boat itself after it started on its way again. And they sang their song to the strokes of their paddles.

The narrow canoe, made from a hollowed-out tree trunk, swayed from side to side, but the boys kept on their feet with perfect balance. They narrowly missed another canoe with three old Negro women in it, but they sang on, undisturbed.

They left the main stream to round the island where the Catholic Mission stood proudly on a hill, then they entered into a branch stream. It was growing late, for they had spent much time taking the baggage off the boat and loading it into the canoe of the older boys. The sun was low, casting its reflection on some houses standing on a rising slope of land. The singing grew louder and merrier as the boys made for a quiet bay to bring their canoe to shore. The older boys followed close behind, singing, too, but not so triumphantly.

The whole mission staff waited at the landing for them, and black hands and white were held out in a greeting of welcome. The doctor and his wife were then escorted to their new home, a bungalow of four small rooms with a veranda on all sides. They could see on one side the glimmering river, widening here and there into a lake, dappled with green islands. There was a glimpse of the main stream, bordered by a range of low hills, deep blue in the fading light. And on the other side of the veranda, not twenty yards away, there was the edge of the primeval forest, somber and mysterious.

There was a brief twilight when the sun sent flares of red and orange through the sky. Then came sudden darkness. A bell rang to call the children to evening prayers and songs in the classroom. Their young voices rose up, loud and clear through the tropical night, with the chirps of crickets and the song of the night birds joining in. Dr. Schweitzer sat on a packing box in his new home and listened silently, deeply moved. But before the song was over, an ugly shadow came creeping slowly down the wall. It was an immense and poisonous spider. Other spiders appeared, and flying beetles as well. They had taken over this house, so long uninhabited, as their own. Now they had to be routed out by the light of an oil lamp before the doctor and his wife could have their well-earned rest and sleep.

All through the night the crickets and frogs kept up their steady chorus, with strange sounds from the forest joining in. There was the clacking of the flying dog, the call of some big ape, an elephant trumpeting in the far distance, or the roar of a hippopotamus to disturb their sleep on this first night in their African home.

At early dawn there was a silence, then when the day broke the sounds of the day commenced. Wild parrots flew screeching and whistling from their roosting places, weaver birds chattered and called in the palms, and there began the lazy drone of millions of midges and flying insects that started with the rising sun.

At six o'clock a bell rang. Soon the voices could be heard of children in the schoolroom, led by the native teacher, Oyembo, whose name meant "The Song." It was time now for the doctor to begin his work. Patients were already waiting outside, even before he could unpack the medical supplies.

Chapter VIII

That everyone shall exert himself in that state of life in which
he is placed, to practice true humanity toward his fellow men, on
that depends the future of mankind.

Out of My Life and Thought

THE NEWS SPREAD from one African village to another, all up
and down the Ogowe River. A white man with the power to
heal, had come to live among them. Oganga, they called him,
which was their word for "fetishman." They came in canoes
and over the jungle trails, bringing their sick for treatment.

Every morning the sound of their chatter could be heard as
they talked in their many tribal languages. There were the
Galoas and Pahouins and other smaller tribes, but the words
of all were strange to European ears. The quick, short syl-
lables were like a song with two notes only.

They were dressed in clothes of all different kinds and colors. Some wore lengths of gay flowered Manchester cloth
wrapped in graceful folds around them, others had on cast-off
European shirts or shorts, ragged, dingy and ill-fitting. And
there were some who had on nothing more than a strip of
woven bark or an animal skin about the middle. Tribal marks
were cut and scarred in patterns on the faces and bodies of
many, and their teeth were filed to sharp points in the way of
cannibals of former times.

There were old men and women, withered like autumn
leaves ready to fall from a tree, some no doubt driven out of
their villages to die because they were of no use to their tribe.
Women were there carrying sick, fretting babies on their

backs, or holding some child by the hand who was covered with painful sores. Well men came supporting a weak or fevered companion, or one wounded by some savage beast from the brush.

Albert Schweitzer saw the truth of the message the missionary had written. Help was indeed badly needed here in the heart of Africa.

"Here among us, we are all sick," a young man told him.

"Our country devours its own people," an old chief remarked.

The mission station had no medical building, but the sick were there, needing help at once and could not be put off until a place was built. The doctor treated his patients out of doors, working in front of his living quarters those first few weeks. The rainy season was on, bringing the usual storm every afternoon, which meant a rush to gather up all the medicines and instruments and seek shelter on the veranda, so the work could be carried on.

A henhouse, built by some former missionary and now abandoned, stood near the doctor's house. It was small and dark, with no window to let in light and air, and it looked as if the slightest puff of wind would blow it away. But at least it had a roof of sorts and would give some kind of protection against the rain and sun, until the medical ward could be built.

The walls of the henhouse were scrubbed and whitewashed, some shelves were built to hold supplies and a camp bed was brought in. This was the first hospital at Lambaréné. Compared to the outdoors, it was a luxury, for now the rains could come pouring down and the doctor could go quietly on with the work of bandaging, giving medicines, or performing minor surgery. In the case of major surgery that could not be postponed, a table was put up in the boys' dormitory. The doctor's wife, with her training as a nurse, was a great help in preparing the instruments and bandages.

One of the patients, who stayed on after he was cured to act as interpreter, also proved himself an able assistant in the medical work. His name was Joseph, and he was one of the Galoa tribe. These people were quick, intelligent and superior to any others of the region. It was from this tribe that the Gullah Negroes of South Carolina are said to have come.

Joseph could speak eight Negro dialects, and he had some knowledge of French and a smattering of English as well. Though he could not read or write, he had a way of remembering the appearance of words on the bottle labels, and never once did he make a mistake when he was asked to bring a certain medicine from the shelf.

He had worked as a cook at Cape Lopez, and it was there that he had picked up his knowledge of French and English. When he was called upon to interpret for a patient describing his symptoms, it was quite natural for him to use such expressions as he had learned in the kitchens.

"Doctor, this man says his leg-of-mutton hurts him," he'd say. Or, "The woman has a pain in her upper left cutlet and also in her loin."

Every morning when he woke up, the doctor found his patients waiting for him, grouped close to the henhouse or standing in the shade of his own cottage. Often as many as thirty or forty a day came in need of treatment. Some had malaria, some had sleeping sickness, and there were those with skin diseases, leprosy, sores caused by the bites of insects. And always there were the ones with broken bones from the attack of a hippopotamus or wounds from a leopard's claws, or from bites and blows from their fellow men.

Marvelous tales were told by the patients returning to their villages after they were healed. Truly the white fetisher had powers greater even than their own fetishmen.

"He knew, without my telling him, that I could scarcely breathe at night and that sometimes my feet were swollen,"

Dr. Schweitzer with school children from the leper colony at Lambaréné

one woman said, after she had been examined with a stethe-
scope for her heart trouble and had been given digitalis to
bring relief.

Anesthetics given in surgery were the cause of much wonder and awe.

"He can kill a person, then cure him, and after that he can
bring the person back to life again," they said of him.

The village witch doctors claimed to have the power to
bring on disease and pain as well as to cure it. It was thought
that Oganga, the white doctor, also had such powers. How
strange it was, the doctor thought when he heard about it,
that he could be looked upon as one who had such power for
good, and yet be thought so dangerous as well.

In the evenings when the day's work was over, and on Sunday afternoons, Albert and Helene Schweitzer went for a
quiet stroll about the mission grounds. They came to know
each foot of it, measuring the length and width with paces.
There were narrow paths leading through the forest where
trees rose like a solid wall almost a hundred feet above their
heads, and so close together not a breath of air could stir
through them. There was a dank and musty smell of earth
and rotted leaves and wood, mingled with the animal smell of
civet cats, monkeys and other creatures hidden in the bushes.

The place had a beauty of its own, though it was as unlike
their own Alsace as any place could possibly be. Sunlight
flecked the leafy shadows, dancing like golden butterflies, and
brilliant-colored birds flitted overhead, quick flashes of green
and orange and vivid blue. But the heat was intolerable to
those who had known the cool pure air of Alsace. They found
it better to stroll down by the sandbanks along the river, as
soon as the dry season began and the waters became low.

During these evening strolls the doctor decided upon the
site where he wanted to build his hospital. It had been planned
for the high ridge close to the boys' dormitory, but there was

too little space there for the kind of hospital he had in mind. The place he chose was on the riverside, near a quiet bay where canoes that brought the sick could land. And it was down the slope near his own cottage where he could be within easy reach, if he were needed in any emergency.

The henhouse was better than no shelter at all, of course, but it was only a makeshift at best and could not serve much longer. There was a desperate need for the new medical building. But it was not until July, three months after the arrival of the doctor, that the Conference of Missionaries was held to approve the site and supply the money needed for the building.

Dr. Schweitzer and the two other missionaries of the station started out one morning before the break of day for the long canoe ride, thirty-five miles up the river, to where the meeting would be held. They sat on folding chairs near the bow of the dugout canoe, one behind the other. Their mattresses and folding camp beds and supplies of food for themselves and the crew were piled in the middle. Toward the stern, twelve men stood in pairs to paddle with their long-handled oars. Another man stood alone at the bow to guide them, and to keep a sharp lookout for shallows, rocks and fallen logs. The men sang as they paddled, making up their song as they went along, in rhythm to their strokes. They sang about the people in the boat and about the place far up the river where they were going. And they sang about how early they had had to get up, before the sun rose in the sky, and about how many hours of rowing they must do before they reached their destination.

They swung out of the side channel into the main stream, just as day was dawning. A silvery mist uncoiled itself and rose in columns to blur the sky and the trees on the horizon. It might have been just such a morning as this at the beginning of creation. There was nothing in sight but water, forest and sky, and no sounds except the song of birds and the splash of the oars—no bells ringing or motors chugging or trolleys clanging.

Suddenly from out of the mist there appeared a row of dark objects moving through the water. The song of the rowers stopped at once as if someone had given a command, for this was a herd of hippopotamuses. They had waddled down from their early morning grazing to romp and bathe in the river. They were immense, some twelve feet long, at least, from upper lip to tail, and almost as tall as a man.

Slowly and quietly the men edged the canoe close to the bank, for though the animals were plunging and splashing like clumsy, giant children at play, the Africans knew well their violent temper if they were disturbed. Tales were told of how they could toss a canoe up in the air as if it were a rubber ball, and how their great jaws could snap off a man's leg or arm in one bite.

The riverbank was not much safer. The current was not so strong there and it was easier to row upstream, but the men had to keep a close watch where the trees dipped their great branches so low they formed a leafy arbor overhead. Pythons might be coiled on any one, ready to spring down into the boat. And crocodiles might be lurking in the shallow water.

It is small wonder the African lives in constant dread and superstitious fear. There is some danger everywhere he turns, in the river, in the jungle and in the sky itself. Malaria-laden mosquitoes droned and hovered over them in the early dawn. And when they disappeared with the rising sun, the tsetse fly came out to replace them. Its sting, which could penetrate the thickest cloth, could bring sleeping sickness and death.

The sun itself became a relentless enemy. Shining down from a cloudless sky, its heat and light were reflected in the water and rose again like flaming arrows piercing through the boat. The men quenched their thirst with fresh, juicy pineapples, and at midday they stopped to rest at a native village where the crew built a fire to roast bananas for their noon meal.

The conference lasted a week, and when it was over the doctor and his companions returned to Lambaréné, their mission accomplished. The proposal for the hospital site had been approved and four hundred dollars given toward the cost of building it.

The journey back was downstream and should have been much quicker, but it was not until after dark that they reached the side channel that brought them to the mission. Twice they had had to cross the river because of herds of threatening hippopotamuses. And when they paddled along the water's edge, they were forced to go slowly, making their way around the sandbanks. Now and then the crew had to get out and push the boat back into deeper water. The song of the rowers grew louder as they came near the landing, then it deepened into a triumphant shout. Lights were seen moving in a zigzag line down the sloping hill. They were the lanterns of the mission people who came to welcome them back.

In his need for the hospital, the doctor was impatient to commence the building right away. With a pointed stick he drew in the dirt where each room of the dormitory should be, and where the beds were to be built. When the workers seemed intolerably slow, he took up a spade and worked beside them. Then he helped saw the heavy logs to the proper size and carry them to the place.

Joseph, the Galoa, gave himself the title of "The First Assistant to the Doctor at Lambaréné." It was true that the doctor had come to rely upon him, knowing that he was doing the best he could. He had learned how to clean and handle the instruments and prepare a patient for surgery. Wearing his long rubber gloves, he stood beside the doctor during the operation. At times, on the rare occasions when the doctor and his wife were called away to treat the sick at some distant mission station, Joseph took charge at home and carried on his duties very well. On one occasion when a man was brought in with an open wound, it was Joseph who made a solution of hydrogen peroxide and biborate of sodium by recognizing the labels on the bottles, and he dressed the wound himself.

"Be sure and lock the medicine room," he always said without fail, even when he knew the doctor would be gone only for a few minutes to see some patient in the dormitory.

"Even from you, Joseph?"

"Even from me. What's not locked up goes for a walk."

With all his intelligence and knowledge of the white man's ways, some of the tribal customs he had grown up with were too much woven within the texture of his life to be rid of easily. He talked often of buying himself a wife, but he would have to have well over a hundred dollars in French francs for the price of one. He could have bought one on the installment plan, but he didn't want to use that method.

"There'd be no peace living with a wife I bought that way," he said. "She would never do a thing I told her, and she'd always make fun of me and say I had no rights over her because she wasn't all paid for."

He had a money box where he kept all his extra earnings, money paid him for sitting up at night or for special services and tips that an occasional white patient, treated at the hospital, might give him. But Joseph was extravagant. It was not easy to save when there were so many tempting things to buy at the markets and trading stores of Lambaréné, such as shoes, sugar and gaily colored ties and shirts.

He saw a pair of patent-leather shoes once, when he went in with the doctor to buy supplies. The shoes were dried and rotting from standing long in a Paris shop window. Like many other odds and ends that could not be sold in Europe, they had been shipped to Africa, where the natives paid far more than they were worth.

The doctor was examining some nails and screws he wanted to buy, when he noticed Joseph standing where the shoes were on display with a look of longing in his eyes. The doctor gave him a warning glance but Joseph paid no attention. Even a nudge in his ribs failed to stop him. At last the doctor gave him a hard pinch on the thigh, so that Joseph took the hint. He put the shoes, which he had been examining, reluctantly aside. On the way back to the mission station the doctor gave him a lecture on thrift, and explained to him that the shoes were not worth the price he would have to pay. Joseph listened good-naturedly and nodded in agreement. But the next day he went alone to Lambaréné and returned to the mission with his patent-leather shoes and an empty money box.

Dr. Schweitzer realized that small differences between the customs and practices of one race and another should not be taken too seriously. He noticed that mothers of newborn babies had themselves and their children painted white all over, to make them look terrifying to the evil spirits. He could even tease, and with a twinkle in his eye he would remind them, as soon as the baby was born, to take care they didn't forget the paint.

The patients were given a round cardboard ticket, hung on a fiber string, each with a number on it. If one had need to come back, the doctor could then look up in his register where he had written the patient's name and the nature of his disease, as well as the medicines given him.

These small pieces of cardboard, worn around the neck and carefully guarded, were looked upon as a kind of fetish such as the village witch doctors made for them to ward off evil spirits. Little bags filled with red feathers, clay, leopard's claws and in some cases bits of human skull of someone killed for that purpose, often dangled on the same string with the cardboard disk.

Dr. Schweitzer saw how these people were pitiful victims of their fears and superstitions, as well as of disease. The gods they worshiped were evil gods. They had no prayers of praise or love or thanks. Their prayers were only offerings and deprecation. They lived in constant dread of some voodoo or evil spell that might be cast upon them, or some taboo, which if broken would surely bring death. Disease itself, they thought, did not happen from any natural cause, but through some evil spirit or a spell cast on them by some human enemy. A worm somehow had been put inside their bodies to eat away the part affected.

"The worm is eating in my stomach," one with stomach pains would say, in describing the symptoms.

The medicine that cured them was a magic charm to make the worm crawl away.

To the doctor, it seemed that there was as great a need to free the minds of these people from their fears and taboos as there was to heal their bodies. He saw many a poor, frightened creature, so dominated by a belief in some taboo that he died of nothing more than a physical and mental shock, because the taboo was broken.

A young man, whose taboo was that he would die if he ever saw the color of his own blood, was brought in wounded by a hippopotamus. The flow of blood was stopped and the wound was treated and began to heal. But he had seen his own blood and nothing could convince him that he would not die. He became a victim of his fears and there was nothing that could be done to save him.

Another youth had as his taboo that he must never eat bananas, or even touch anything that had been put in a pot where bananas were cooked. He learned once that some fish he had eaten had been cooked in a pot with a few leftover bananas still in it. He was seized with convulsions as soon as he heard the news, and died a short while after. A woman, whose taboo was that her first-born must be a boy, died in the same way, when a girl was born.

Many times a human life was saved at the hospital through other means than medicine. Two men had been fishing on the river when they were attacked by a hippopotamus. The beast had hurled the canoe up in the air, and one of the men managed to escape unhurt. The other was badly wounded, and had been chased about in the water at least a half hour before he finally managed to drag himself up on the river-bank.

Twelve hours later he was brought to the hospital, after the witch doctor had tried his magic and failed. There was no hope for the victim, in spite of the treatment he received. Before he breathed his last, his brother turned to take revenge upon the fishing companion, who had come to the hospital also.

Joseph drew the doctor aside and explained to him the law of the jungle. The companion who had survived owned the boat they had gone fishing in. It was he who had suggested going in the first place. Now he was considered responsible for the accident and death. That was why he had come with the victim to the hospital. And it was why the dead man's relatives were planning to take him back to the village, by force if necessary, to stand trial.

"His life will be in danger when they do take him back," Joseph said.

Dr. Schweitzer saw the fear in the face of the unfortunate man, as he tried to break away from his captors.

"I am keeping this man on here as a worker," the doctor announced, and he demanded his release.

The relatives of the dead man protested. They promised to

give him a fair trial, but Joseph, knowing the ways of his countrymen, put no trust in the words.

"They will kill him without fail," he insisted.

The doctor stayed beside the riverbank until the canoe carrying the victim and his relatives was well on its way, to make sure they did not slip back and drag the survivor with them by force.

Through Joseph's eyes Dr. Schweitzer had his first glimpse into the mystery of this strange land. These people were not acting through any cruel motives, he realized. It was simply a duty, sacred to them, to see that one even so remotely responsible for the death of another should atone for it. A life for a life, they wanted. The doctor recognized and understood their strong sense of justice. But this was one case, he decided, that would have to be taken to the District Court at Lambaréné, where it could be settled in orderly fashion.

The medicine men used every means possible without hesitation to keep their authority over the people. It was through Joseph again that Dr. Schweitzer learned of this. He had heard about the fishing expedition held every year in the middle of the dry season, when the waters of the Ogowe were low. The whole village went off to a sandbank about three hours' journey upstream, where they lived for two weeks. They built an arbor of tree branches for shelter, and they had fish to eat for every meal, boiled, baked or stewed. All that was left over they dried and smoked and took back to the village.

"And you, Joseph," Dr. Schweitzer said, for he was reminded by it of the Old Testament harvest festivals, when the people rejoiced before Yahweh. "Don't you want to go with them?"

Joseph was so fond of fishing his eyes nearly popped out of the sockets at the very mention of it. But he showed no enthusiasm over the offer of a vacation just then. He wasn't in a hurry, he said. He'd wait a little while, then later on he would go.

The doctor wanted to know why, and the reason for his reluctance came out. There was no fishing done on the first day, he said. Instead, the place was blessed by the elders. They poured rum and threw tobacco leaves into the water to put the evil spirits in a good humor so they would let the fish be caught in the nets.

"But surely you don't believe in such magic," Dr. Schweitzer said in surprise.

"No," Joseph answered. "But if anyone dares to say a word against these beliefs, or even smile while the rum and tobacco are being offered, sooner or later he's sure to be punished. The medicine men never forgive. And sometimes we don't even know ourselves which one of the elders is the real medicine man."

Joseph was taking no chances. He stayed on at the hospital until the fishing was well under way, then went off in his canoe and enjoyed himself with the rest of his tribe.

With patience and understanding, the doctor tried to combat such superstitions and fears.

Now that there was a hospital to take them in, orphan babies could be kept and cared for, fed on canned milk from Europe, until they were able to eat the food of the adults. The old came, too, turned out of their own villages because they were sick and feeble and no longer useful to the tribe.

"Don't take in these people you know will die," Joseph advised time and again. "None of the village fetishmen would think of such a thing. It would ruin their reputation if a patient died while they were treating him."

Many a poor dying creature, turned away by the witch doctors and abandoned by his own people, managed somehow to make his way to Albert Schweitzer's hospital, or was brought in stealthily by night and left there.

"Let them come," the doctor said. "They are all welcome. My hospital is open to all sufferers."

Those who could not be saved from death could at least be shown love and tenderness, and the end would be a little easier for them. He would spare them as much pain as he could.

Joseph was right in one thing, however. In Africa, he could be honest with his patients. When he knew there was no hope for a cure, he could explain it gently, instead of giving false hopes and pretending. Death, to the African, has always been something as natural as birth. He can face it calmly when the time actually comes.

A doctor needs to conserve his emotional strength and energy, so he can give the same attention to all. But try as he would, Dr. Schweitzer could not put from his mind the immense pity and anxiety he felt for each patient. He suffered with them in their pain and weakness. To him it had been well worth any amount of sacrifice or discomfort, well worth all the years of study and preparation to come here, just to see the joy of those who had been plagued with sores, after they had been cleanly bandaged so they no longer had to drag their poor bleeding feet through the mud. And sweeter than any music was the contented cooing of a baby that had been crying in pain.

Akewa the word that meant "thank you," was often heard. Many wanted to show their gratitude by bringing gifts, or offering what little money they could afford. One payment that meant a great deal was labor done for the hospital. An uncle of a boy that had been brought in covered with sores spent fourteen days making cupboards for the hospital out of packing boxes. A black trader offered the services of his workers, so that the roof of the doctor's own cottage could be repaired.

The greatest reward of all came when, after an operation

was over and the patient had regained consciousness, the doctor felt a hand reach out for his own and cling to it. And it was with joy he heard the words, "I've no more pain! I've no more pain!"

It was at times such as this, he wrote in his report of that year, that he and his patients could sit side by side and feel that they knew by experience the meaning of the words, "And all ye are brethren."

Chapter IX

The ways along which we have to struggle toward the goal may
be veiled in darkness, yet the direction in which we must travel
is clear.

The Philosophy of Civilization

THE SEASONS came and passed. They were not the seasons of
Alsace which Albert and Helene Schweitzer had known before, seasons of bud and leaf and seeds in pod. There were no
long and lingering twilights of summer when the sun seemed
reluctant to set and the afterglow stayed on in the sky for
hours. And there was no winter, with the blaze and crackle of
wood fires and snowflakes softly falling on a windowpane.
The days were even and always warm in their African home,
and flowers bloomed the year round in open places, where
they could catch the sun. The forest was the same deep,
matted green, never changing. On one tree alone there could
be new buds and blossoms and ripening fruit at the same time.
They counted time instead by dry seasons and wet ones.

It had been near the end of the rainy season when the
Schweitzers had first arrived in Africa. By the last of May
the rains stopped. The sky became colorless and cloudless,
and the sun shone sullenly through an opaque and milk-white
heat mist. They saw the river recede. Islands of sand, hidden
until then, appeared like the bones of a lean and hungry animal. This was the time of the year when the crocodiles could
be seen dozing like so many logs of wood along the riverbank. And hippopotamuses gathered in the late evening on

their favorite island, where the channel met the main stream, to splash and snort and play in the water. This was the time of the year, too, when little native children coughed and sniffled, and old men's bones ached with rheumatism, for the nights were chilly during the dry season. A straw mat for a bed on a hard dirt floor, with no more covering than the few rags they wore during the day, brought little sleep to the African in his village hut.

"I'm going to double up my legs," was the expression used by some of the tribes, when a man spoke of going to sleep at night. But in the heat of midday, when he could make up for the sleep he had lost at night, he said of his noon siesta, "I'm going to stretch out my legs."

The dry season lasted four months, until the beginning of October, and then came the rains, to last the other eight months of the year. The wind rose every evening then, roaring, buoyant, to shake and toss the trees. And the rain came piercing down, soaking into the earth and seeping through to the dirt floors of all the village huts. Even when the sun came out the next morning, there was still a heavy moisture in the air, and leaves on the bushes glistened with drops left from the night before. The river rose quickly. Mango trees, palms and the gray-trunked okoume seemed then to have left the high bank where they had been standing only a day or so before, to go like children wading in the water. Their branches dipped low to form a green roof for the passing canoes.

There was another dry season and now it was drawing to a close, the second one the doctor and his wife had seen since their arrival in Africa. It was time to begin making plans for a vacation back home in Alsace. They would go before the next dry season set in, they decided. After two years in the tropics, they would need to recruit their strength and health in a cooler, better climate.

There had often been times of discouragement and exasperation since the doctor's arrival. And he could think of so much yet to be done. Yet he looked back with some satisfaction on all that had been accomplished in the past sixteen months. The little hospital had been built from the ground up. Two thousand patients had been treated and healed before there was scarcely time to feel settled in it. And every day more were added. It had truly been worth while coming here. And the sacrifices he had been prepared to make were not as great as he had expected.

He had come to the heart of Africa to live, forgotten and unknown except to the sick and the needy who came to him for help. And he had been prepared to give up the three things that had meant much to him, his lecturing, preaching and the music he loved.

But the Bach Society of Paris had given him a piano to bring with him when he left Europe. It was lined with metal to protect it from termites and mildew, and it had the pedals of an organ so he could keep in practice. For a long time he had not had the heart to touch it. When it was brought up from the landing still in its packing box, he had watched anxiously. There were so many carriers that it seemed to have sprouted legs and heads in rows on each side. He saw that it was uncrated carefully, but when it was brought into the house and put in place he looked at it for a moment, then turned away. No, he thought. Better to let his fingers and feet go rusty with disuse, as he had said when he left Europe. Too much needed to be done here. There would be no time for music.

One night, weary from the day's work, the doctor sat down at the piano and began fingering the keys. Scarcely realizing what he was doing, he began on a Bach fugue, while his feet worked the pedals as if on an organ. Then, in the gloomy stillness of his forest home, he played on and on. There was no need to give up his music. He would use his free time, even if it were only a half hour out of a busy day, trying to make his technique as deep and perfect as he could. He would take only one piece at a time, something by Bach, by Mendelssohn, Widor, César Franck, and study each one carefully, down to the smallest detail. He would go over them, one by one, until he knew them all by heart. There would be no rush now, no concerts to prepare for, no time schedules to meet. He could take his time, quietly. And music would come to mean more than ever to him because of it. This was a beginning. It led him back to work he had started long before and had thought he would have to give up. With renewed interest, he set to work again on an American edition of the volumes he had written on the music of Bach.

Before having been allowed to come to Africa, Dr. Schweitzer had had to agree to practice medicine only, and do no preaching. This had been brought about because his search for truth had led him to express some ideas in his books which were considered too liberal by members of the Board of Missions in Paris.

"I'll be as silent as a carp," he had promised.

But he found that the men who had come to Africa to bring Christianity to the people could not let themselves be held back by questions of dogma. If they were to be understood by their listeners, they had to go back to the simplicity of the Gospel. And it was not long after the doctor's arrival that he was asked to take part in the services. He would not have to give up preaching, after all.

It was a wonderful experience to be able to bring a religion of love to people who had known only a religion of fear and cruelty. And what better way could there be to teach them than with the words of Jesus in His Sermon on the Mount, or through the early sayings of the apostle Paul?

The teacher Oyembo, whose name meant "the Song,"

helped him by interpreting his sermons in the language of the people. On Saturday evening he would come to the doctor's house and together they would go over the sermon, phrase by phrase, and discuss it. If there was some expression which the people could not understand, such as *vineyard* or "field of corn," Oyembo suggested something that was familiar to them to take its place.

There was a bond between these two men, one from a little village deep in the jungle and the other from seats of learning in European capitals. Dr. Schweitzer looked upon Oyembo as one of the finest men of all his wide acquaintance. Seldom had one been so well named, he thought, for Oyembo had made of his life a fine melody.

Many of the youths of Africa, after receiving their education at the mission schools, thought of one thing only, to go away from their native villages and seek some clerical job in the government, or work behind the counter in some store in a larger town. But Oyembo had seen the needs of his own people. He had chosen to stay on, because he wanted to help his people to a better way of life, though as a teacher in a mission school he was poorly paid, and the work was not easy. Such men as Oyembo, and his wife who was equally bright, and their three well-brought-up children, gave promise to the future of Africa. Enough families like these could make the continent great.

"What is it like, this country of the whites?" the doctor was often asked by the Africans. "How is it different from our own?"

The difference was so vast in some ways that it was not possible to explain. And yet in other ways, when one considered men like Oyembo, both places were much the same.

Once on a canoe trip the men at the oars asked the question again.

"What is it like in the country you came from?"

"For one thing," the doctor answered, looking at the dark, somber forest standing like a high green wall on each side of the river, "we have great forest fires sometimes, when the wind is high and there has been little rain."

He told of how the living trees would blaze high, with flames spreading quickly from one to the other, until the whole forest was afire. This was something almost impossible to imagine for those living in such a humid climate. Even in the dry season it was hard enough to burn logs that had been cut down and seasoned when land had been cleared for a banana plantation. But living trees! How could they ever burn?

"Another thing," the doctor said, with a twinkle in his eye, for now he knew their language enough to understand the song they had been singing about how hard they had to work paddling the canoe. "There are men in my country who go out in a canoe just for pleasure."

"Even when they don't have to make a journey?" the men asked. "And when they have no goods to haul?"

What other reason could a man possibly have to go out in a boat and row?

"They go for the sport of it. Because they want the exercise," the doctor answered.

The men laughed at the very thought of people so foolish as to do physical labor such as paddling a canoe when they didn't have to. Surely the doctor was exaggerating.

"What other difference?" they wanted to know.

The doctor thought of Joseph, still putting money in his money box to save for a wife, and still spending it for something he couldn't resist buying.

"The men get married there without having to pay for their wives," he said.

The men shook their heads at this. No, it couldn't be true. The doctor was teasing and having a little joke at their expense, because he thought they didn't know any better. Who ever heard of a man getting married without having to pay the wife's family the money they asked!

Europe seemed far away then, in the summer of 1914. There had been no news since the beginning of July and now it was well into August, but no one thought much about it, for the boats were slow and the mail was weeks in coming. Time mattered little in the heart of Africa then. Each day was the same, with the sick to be treated and the young to be fed and clothed and taught. Suddenly then, there came the news of war—a war that was to be felt all over the world, even to the remotest place.

The doctor had prepared some medicine for a sick woman at Cape Lopez, and he sent it to the store at Lambaréné by Joseph, with a request that they send it by their boat on its next trip down the river.

Joseph came back with a short note that read:

> In Europe they are mobilizing and are probably already at war. We must place our boat at the disposal of the authorities and cannot say when it will go next to Cape Lopez.

News came the next day that war had been declared. And that very evening, Dr. Schweitzer and his wife were told that they must now consider themselves prisoners of war.

Although Alsace had once been part of the French Republic, it had been taken by the Germans five years before Dr. Schweitzer's birth. He and his wife were German citizens because of it, and here, in a French Colony, they were looked upon as enemy aliens. They would be allowed to stay on in the house they were occupying, they were told, but they must have no communication with either the whites or the blacks. Native soldiers, in their navy blue shorts and tunics, and tasseled red fezzes on their heads, were sent to the mission to stand guard at their door and see that the orders were obeyed.

The doctor found it strange to wake up in the early morning, knowing that he must stay indoors, unable to go down to the hospital to see how the sick had fared during the night. He found himself often sitting at his piano for solace. Would he ever see Europe again, he wondered. And if he did, what kind of Europe would it be? He thought of the young men of both France and Germany, many lying in trenches, wounded and in pain. Was this where civilization had led, and was it the beginning of its downfall? He began to write down the thoughts that came to him, though he knew there was a chance that everything he wrote would be taken away, since he was a prisoner of war.

The Africans could not understand the meaning of this sudden internment of their doctor. They scolded the native guards. What did they mean, setting themselves as masters of the Grand Docteur, telling him what he could and could not do? The Europeans added their objections also, for they saw no good reason why they should be denied the services of the only doctor within hundreds of miles. Scarcely a day passed that the District Commandant didn't find himself having to send a note to the guards, telling them to let the bearer see the doctor because he needed treatment. This continued for three months until, through the intercession of the faithful Charles Widor in Paris, the Schweitzers were released from their internment and work in the hospital could go on once more.

News of the war began coming in fairly regularly. Messages were telegraphed from Cape Lopez or Libreville to the District Commandant at Lambaréné every two weeks. And he, in turn, sent the news by a native soldier to the stores and to the Catholic and Protestant mission stations.

"Everything costs more now," Joseph started to complain

one day, while he was helping the doctor as he bandaged the wounds of a patient.

"You shouldn't talk that way, Joseph," the doctor answered. "Don't you see how the faces of the doctor and his wife and the other missionaries here are troubled? War means much more to us than a rise in prices. We are all grieved about our fellow men, wounded and dying on the battlefield."

Joseph looked at him in astonishment, as if he were realizing for the first time some meaning that had been hidden from him.

News came of the death of one after another of the white men who had left this region of Africa to fight on the battlefields of Europe.

"So many men already killed in the war!" an old African exclaimed in surprise, when he heard that ten were dead. He was not aware that there were many thousands from other places added to them. "Why don't their tribes meet to talk out the palaver? How can they ever pay for all those dead men!"

In native warfare, which the old man remembered from his youth, all who fall, whether among the victors or the conquered, had to be paid for by the other side. Another thing that concerned him was that since the Europeans did not eat the warriors slain in battle, why then should they want to kill so many, unless it was out of sheer cruelty?

There were others who came to the doctor in bewilderment, asking how it was that the whites, with their religion of love, were now murdering each other. Dr. Schweitzer did not even attempt to explain.

"We are in front of something terrible which one cannot understand," was all that he could say.

That Christmas a small palm was brought into the house for their Christmas tree. Bright ornaments were hung on its branches and the candles were lit at twilight, giving a soft and cheerful glow to the room. They flickered in the night breeze, sending dancing shadows over the walls and in the corners.

The war could be forgotten for a little while, as the group at the mission station gathered together, French citizens, German citizens and Africans, to sing Christmas carols and exchange small gifts. Outside, the mango trees and kapoks rustled gently with the wind in their branches, and beyond the Ogowe flowed, silent and serene. The stars shone palely down, the Great Bear and the Southern Cross and the clusters that formed the Milky Way. It was on just such a still, calm night as this, and not too far to the north of where they were, that the angels sang so long ago to the shepherds as they watched their flocks:

Glory to God in the highest, and on earth peace, good will toward men.

When the candles on the tree had burned to half their length, the doctor blew them out.

"But why?" his wife asked.

"They're all we have," Dr. Schweitzer answered. "We'd better save them for next year."

"For next year?"

She shook her head sadly. Who could tell what next year would bring?

What a mercy it was, the doctor felt, that while so many men found it their duty to bring suffering and death to others, he was able to ease pain and save human lives. A shipment of medical supplies, which had left Europe just before war was declared, managed to get through to Lambaréné. This meant the work could go on, for there were several cases of drugs and bandages. But these would have to last a long time. Who could tell when another shipment could be sent?

Food was more of a problem then than medicine, for herds of elephants roamed over the land, eating the bananas and trampling down the manioc plants. A herd of twenty could destroy a whole plantation in a single night and bring many months of hunger to the village. No one knew when they came, for, big and cumbersome though they were, they had a way of moving as silently as the whispering wind. And they could cover their tracks by lifting branches with their trunks and tossing them behind. During the day they stayed hidden in the swamps of the deep forest, and came by night to the places they had reconnoitered beforehand.

"Now if we were with Mr. Cadier, he'd have shot us a couple of monkeys and some birds so we could have meat," some of the Africans complained one day when they were in a canoe with the doctor. "But you pass right up close to a crocodile and never even touch your gun. Nothing ever happens when we are with you."

Dr. Schweitzer saw the water birds circling and swooping gracefully to skim the surface of the river and he could not bring himself to kill one. Nor would he shoot a monkey swinging in the high branches of a tree, an easy target for any hunter. It happened often that one was wounded only, and fell in the underbrush where it was impossible to reach. Worse still it might become tangled in the leafy branches, to die a slow and painful death. Even if one found the body, there was a chance of finding also a baby monkey, whimpering and clinging pitifully to its dying mother.

The war in Europe was felt around the world, even to the remotest places in the heart of Africa. Not only were the people affected by the rise in prices, the scarcity of food and the shortage of labor in the timber camps. But soon men of the Ogowe River were being drafted into service as carriers for the military colony of the Cameroons.

"Is it still war, Doctor?" Aloys, the cook, asked every time the mail came in.

"Yes, Aloys, still war."

"Oh la la!" Aloys mumbled with a shake of his head. "Oh la la! Oh la la!"

At N'Gomo, a village between Cape Lopez and Lambaréné, a group of carriers were put on board a river steamer to be taken to their post. The doctor, who had been called there to treat the wife of one of the missionaries, stood on the riverbank to watch the boat depart. A group of women were gathered, wailing over sons and husbands who were being taken away. They saw the boat move slowly on, until the last trail of smoke disappeared far in the distance, then when they could see no more they went on their way. One old woman stayed on, sitting alone on a stone and weeping silently over this thing which she could not understand. Dr. Schweitzer went up to her and took her hand, trying to think of words to comfort her. But she went on crying as if she did not hear, or even know that he was there. Suddenly he felt that he, too, was crying with her, toward the empty river and the setting sun.

He had come on this journey on a little steamer towing a loaded barge. Seated on the deck of the barge, he had been thinking about how the civilized nations of the world were waging war against each other. What could be done to prevent absolute destruction of the civilization built up through all the past years? The solution was not in turning one's back upon the world and becoming lost in contemplation only of higher things. After all we are in the world and part of it, and if one progresses spiritually, it must be through an acceptance, and not a denial, of the world. Some ideal to work toward was needed, something that would make the world a better place to live in. But the fire of man's ideals was burning low. Some new method of thought was needed to get back to the true ideals of civilization.

As the doctor sat thinking of these things, he looked up to see a herd of hippopotamuses bathing and cavorting in the water. They parted at the approach of the boat, some going one way and some another. It was at the hour of sunset, when a band of sparkling gold was reflected in the river, and the whole sky seemed to have caught the heat of the day and held it, flaming red, for a few last moments.

"I am life which wills to live, in the midst of life which wills to live."

This thought had been with him since he was a child, before even he could find the words to express it. Every living creature had the desire to live, just as he had. And every living creature had that same right.

Reverence for Life. The phrase came to him then, unlooked for, unexpected. If all mankind could have that reverence for life, not only for his own, but for others too, there was hope for a glorious civilization to come.

After his return to the mission station and his hospital there, he began to write again on the book he had started about civilization and ethics. Every evening when the work of caring for the sick was over, Dr. Schweitzer sat at his table beside the lattice door leading out on the veranda. Beneath the table a baby antelope lay curled at his feet sleeping peacefully. Outside, his dog Caramba gave a low growl now and then at some strange cry from the jungle, a gorilla perhaps, or a leopard in search of prey, just to let him know she was on guard. Here in this solitude, with the light of an oil lamp shedding its soft glow on the papers before him, the doctor set down the thoughts that had been going through his head for a long time.

"As in my will to live there is ardent desire for further life, and for the mysterious exaltation of the will to live which we call pleasure, while there is fear of destruction and of that mysterious lessening of the will to live which we call pain, so are these in the will to live around me, whether it can express itself to me or remains dumb."

The evening wind blew gently through the lattice door. Outside the crickets chirped and the palm trees swayed with a rustling sound. The sleepy antelope stirred and the doctor reached down to stroke it. He glanced at the clock. Before nine he must go down to the hospital for a last look at his patients, to see that they were resting comfortably. Many would be waiting on their cots under the mosquito nets to hear his words as he passed by, "Good night. Sleep well."

. "The ideal of *Reverence for Life* holds within itself everything that can be described as love, devotion and sympathy, whether in suffering, joy or effort."

Blessed solitude of the primeval forest, he called it. How could he ever thank it enough for what it had meant to him!

Christmas came again, and the half candles left from the year before burned down to the sockets on the decorated palm tree.

The money which the doctor had brought with him, enough, he had thought, to keep the hospital going for two years, was fast dwindling and debts were piling up. Medical supplies were pitifully low, and food was scarce. There was some canned milk for the babies, but when that was gone no one could tell when more could be sent.

Joseph left the hospital. It was not possible to go on paying him the salary he had been receiving.

"My dignity would not allow me to work for less money than I've been getting," he said.

He went back to live with his parents in his native village, which was on the island across the river channel. He took his money box with him, with forty dollars in it he had managed to save toward the price of a wife. But little by little it went the way the money before had gone, for things needed or that had caught his fancy in the stores of Lambaréné. And married life was still far in the future for him.

Oyembo also left the mission station. With a wife and three

growing children to support, it had been hard enough to make ends meet on a teacher's small pay. Now, with the rising prices and the still smaller salary the mission had to offer, he was forced to go out and look for work elsewhere.

Still another war Christmas came. The little palm tree was decorated with ornaments, but there were no candles to brighten it. This was the third since the war started and still there was not even a rumor of peace. The sick still came and now there were the Europeans added to their numbers, missionaries from other stations, traders and timber merchants, prevented by the war from returning to their homes. Often the doctor gave up his own bed for some patient and slept on a screened-in part of the veranda.

The midday hour of rest, between lunch and two o'clock when work in the hospital commenced again, was a time of music for the doctor. He went over the organ pieces of Bach until he felt he could enter into the spirit of their meaning with more ease and appreciation than ever before. And in the evenings after supper, until nine o'clock when he went down for his nightly visit to the hospital, he worked on the book. It was beginning to take shape now, and he had given it the title of *Philosophy of Civilization*.

The rainy season drew to a close. This was the time the driver ants began their march. They came out twice a year, at the beginning and at the end of the rainy season. Like soldiers in formation, they appeared, five or six abreast and in perfect order. Across a path or in an open space, the huge black warrior ants took up their posts as guards, lined up in rows on each side of the column. They stood for hours, with their backs to the procession and their heads, with powerful jaws almost as large as the rest of the body, facing a possible enemy. Secure in their protection, the smaller ants scurried past, carrying their young with them. They rushed so fast that sometimes a warrior ant found himself swept off his feet and taken along like a wood chip on a river current. Then he righted himself and took up his post again.

These ants have a way of suddenly breaking column to disperse, as if at some secret signal. In the twinkling of an eye, they become a quivering black mass spreading out over the ground, to devour every living thing within reach that cannot make its escape. Crickets in the grass, snakes that cannot crawl away quickly enough, beetles, frogs, mice, civet cats, all fall prey to them. Even the big spiders in the trees do not escape, for the ants can crawl up to the highest limb. And if one should try to get away by jumping, there are others on the ground ready to pounce on it.

The doctor's house lay in the path of their semiannual foraging, and more than once he was awakened at night by the warning sound of chickens in the henhouse, clucking and scratching. If there was also a sudden hush of other night noises, crickets and frogs and night birds silenced, he knew the ants were on the march again. He had to rush quickly to open the henhouse door so the chickens could escape, while his wife took down the bugle from the wall and blew three times upon it. This brought help from among the patients at the hospital who were able to get up, or their families that had accompanied them. Buckets of water were brought up from the river and mixed with Lysol, which was sprinkled around and under the house by lantern light. The warrior ants rushed to the defense, creeping over the doctor and the men working with him. Their bite was fierce, with the jaws digging in and clinging so hard that, even if they were pulled off and the bodies broken, the jaws stayed on in the flesh and had to be taken out separately.

At the smell of Lysol the ants moved on to another place, once more in marching columns guarded by the warriors, only to disperse again where they were safe from attack.

The African knew these creatures well. At the first sign of

their approach, the whole family took up their sleeping mats and left the hut, turning it over to the ants. They knew that eventually, when the ants had gone, they would return to find their houses cleaned of all vermin, cockroaches, mice and even any mamba snakes that might have been lurking in the thatched roof.

"The world, however, offers us a horrible drama of Will to Live divided against itself," the doctor wrote. "One existence holds its own at the cost of another; one destroys another. Only in thinking man has the Will to Live become aware of other will to live.

"Even man, with a reverence for the life of others, often finds himself obliged to live at the cost of other life," he went on. "Again and again man is forced to bring upon himself the guilt of destroying or injuring life, to save his own or to save the life of another creature. He tries to avoid this necessity whenever it is possible, he longs to preserve his own humanity and to bring to other lives some release from their suffering."

More than three years in the tropics, with the meager wartime diet, began to show its effect upon the doctor's wife. He was also in need of a rest and a change of air. A timber merchant, whose wife had been cured of an illness at the hospital, offered the Schweitzers a cottage at his campsite near Cape Lopez, at the mouth of the Ogowe. It had been the home of the men who had looked after the timber rafts, but since the war had started, when the shipping of timber was no longer possible, it had stood empty.

The change was good for both the doctor and his wife. They were revived by the cool, clean air blowing in from the sea. There was an abundance of fish in the bay, and every day they had fresh herrings for their dinner.

A few laborers had stayed on, for there were still some rafts of lumber in the bay. Dr. Schweitzer went out to join the men in their work. They loosened the heavy okoume logs which had been bound together, and rolled them up on dry land where they would be safe from boreworms. It would be a long while before a cargo of this wood was ever shipped again for the plywood of Europe and America.

One evening the doctor went out for a stroll and passed a group of abandoned huts, built at a time when there were many more laborers on the place. They were falling to ruins now, used only as a sleeping place for tribes that passed that way, needing shelter for the night. Dr. Schweitzer called out to see if any happened to be occupied, but there was no answer. Then he opened the doors, to make sure. In the last hut he saw a man lying on the dirt floor, his head almost buried in the dust and sand. He was covered with ants.

The man was still breathing, but the doctor saw at once that he was a victim of sleeping sickness, and had been left there to die, unable to go farther.

Dr. Schweitzer knelt down beside the man and did all he could to make him clean and comfortable in his last hours. Through the open door of the hut he could see the clear blue water of the bay, set in a frame of green woods. It was a scene of magic beauty, with the setting sun pouring down its golden, shimmering light upon it. To be shown in one single glance such beauty and such hopeless, helpless misery was overwhelming. This was Africa, he thought, in all its poetry and its prose.

Chapter X

Anyone who proposes to do good must not expect people to roll stones out of the way, but must accept his lot calmly if they even roll a few more upon it.

Out of My Life and Thought

THREE YEARS had passed since that August day when the message was brought, telling of the war that had broken out in Europe, and there was still no hope for peace. Except for the first three months when Dr. Schweitzer and his wife were kept under guard in their home, the work of caring for the sick had gone on at Lambaréné, Cape Lopez, N'Gomo, or wherever he was called. Suddenly the order came that these two were to be taken to Europe, as prisoners of war. A boat was due any time, the message said, and they must be ready to leave with no more notice.

There was a rush of gathering up all their belongings and packing them in crates. Their neighbors, the French missionaries, came to help them, and also an American who was staying there at the time. They nailed down covers on the crates containing the last of the medicines and the medical supplies and bandages, and put them in a small building of corrugated iron, where they would be safe.

The doctor took up his manuscript and looked it over. He decided against taking it with him, for it would no doubt be confiscated, and the work of these past two years would be lost.

"Will you keep this for me until the war is over?" he asked the American, Mr. Ford.

The man agreed, and accepted the heavy pile of papers, written in German about the philosophy of civilization. He would keep it out of friendship, he said, though he had his doubts as to whether or not it was the right thing to do.

The doctor had hastily made a brief outline of the book in French, working late in the night over it, and he packed this to take with him in case his finished work was lost.

Luckily, the boat was late in arriving, which gave time for a few last-minute things to be done. A man was brought in from one of the neighboring villages for an emergency operation. And there were instructions to give to the sick before they were sent back to their homes. What would become of them now, the doctor wondered.

When the boat arrived and pulled up to the landing place at Lambaréné, native guards escorted Dr. Schweitzer and his wife on board. The Father Superior of the French Catholic Mission came up the gangplank, waving aside the guards that tried to hold him back.

"You shall not leave this country without my thanking you both for all the good you've done," he said, shaking hands with the doctor and his wife.

Albert and Helene stood on the deck of the little river boat to wave good-by to the people that had gathered to see them off. There were the French co-workers in the mission, the American, Mr. Ford, and the Father Superior in his white robe and helmet. They were citizens of countries waging war against each other, but it had not changed the loyalty and friendship they felt for each other.

There were the Negroes also, for whom all of them had come to Africa. They stood close to the water, shouting their farewells as the boat moved slowly on. Long after their faces were blurred by distance, the color of their garments stood out, in gay reds and blues and yellows, blending with the dark brown of almost naked bodies of those who had come

Portrait of Dr. Schweitzer, 1952

from deep in the jungle. There were a few with only plain dingy white cloth wrapped in folds around them like Lazarus in his winding sheet.

How many thousands had come and gone from the hospital since it was first started four and a half years ago. They passed through the doctor's thoughts as the boat glided on down the river. There was the old couple, the leper and his wife, who had rowed for two hundred and fifty miles upstream in a canoe, because they had heard of Oganga, the white medicine man who had such magic charm to cure. And there was the old couple who had come during the famine, sick and half starved because they had not eaten for two days. And the little boy so terrified that he had to be carried by force into the examining room. It was learned later that he was sure the doctor meant to kill and eat him, as men still did in the village he came from.

When the river boat reached Cape Lopez, a Frenchman whose wife had been cured at the Lambaréné hospital came up to the doctor and offered him some money in case he had none. Again and again, through such little things as that, the doctor saw how, in spite of wars and the hatred and cruelty that resulted from them, there was a goodness in the hearts of men that nothing could change.

When they boarded the ocean liner that was to take them back to Europe, they were taken to their cabin, and orders were given that they must not see or talk to anyone except the steward assigned to them. This steward, whose name was Gaillard, brought their food to them and took them up on deck at certain hours for air and exercise. During the long hours in between, the doctor filled the time by memorizing some of Bach's fugues and Widor's Sixth Organ Symphony. He practiced with his fingers on the table, pretending it was an organ, as he used to do when he was a child too small to reach the keys. And he used the bare floor for pedals.

"Have you noticed the way I've treated you?" Gaillard, the steward, said one day toward the end of the voyage. "Not many prisoners of war have been treated so well, you know. Now about your meals, I've always served them with everything nice and clean. And there's never been any more dirt left in your cabin than in any of the others'."

The doctor admitted that he was right, wondering what was coming next.

"Can you guess why I did this?" the man went on. "It wasn't because I expected a tip—not from a prisoner of war. I'll tell you why. A few months ago a man named Gaucher traveled back to France on this ship in one of my cabins. 'Gaillard,' he said to me, 'it may happen that before long you'll be taking the doctor from Lambaréné to Europe as a prisoner of war on this ship. If that happens, I want you to promise, for my sake, you'll help him in every way you can.' He had been a patient in your hospital, he told me, and he said you'd cured him. And now," the steward added with a smile, "you know why I treated you so well."

The ship landed at Bordeaux, and the doctor with his wife stepped foot on European soil for the first time in almost five years. It was a far different homecoming than the one they had dreamed of when they first left, thinking to return for their vacation in two years.

They were put in temporary barracks with others from enemy countries. After three weeks they were sent to a place in the Pyrenees Mountains near the Spanish border. Two gendarmes came in a carriage at midnight to take them away. The order telling them they should be ready to leave had only come that night, and the doctor, weak now with pain and fever, had misunderstood, thinking they meant the following night. And he had waited for morning light before beginning to pack.

The gendarmes were furious to find what they took to be

an act of disobedience. They stood waiting impatiently, while the doctor and his wife tried to collect all their belongings in the feeble light of a lantern, and stuff them into trunks. Once the gendarmes threatened to take them on without the baggage if they didn't move faster.

Dr. Schweitzer made a secret vow to himself as he went on with his packing. "If ever I've been impatient with others," he thought, "from this night on, no matter what cause I might have, I shall never lose my patience again."

The gendarmes took pity in the end, and even gave a helping hand themselves in the packing, searching for books and clothes and bottles of medicine to put in the trunk.

When the doctor and his wife reached the camp in the Pyrenees, the trunks were opened and everything taken out to be examined.

"Now what is this?" a guard said, holding up a French translation of Aristotle's *Politics*. "Think of it!" he stormed. "Bringing books on politics into a prisoner of war camp!"

"That is the translation of a book written long before the birth of Christ," the doctor ventured to explain.

"Is that true, you scholar there?" the guard asked another man standing near.

The man nodded and said it was true.

"What! People talked politics as long ago as that!" the guard exclaimed.

"Yes," the doctor and the scholar answered.

"Oh well, as far as I'm concerned, you can keep the book. I don't suppose they talked politics then the way we talk it now."

The guard put the book back into the trunk, and he quickly passed over the rest of the contents, letting all through. The outline of his book on philosophy which the doctor had translated into French was spared. And he was allowed to keep the supply of medicines he had brought with him.

The place where they had come was once a monastery where sick people made pilgrimages from far and near, hoping to be cured. It had stood empty and slowly falling to ruins since the government had taken it over many years ago. Now a strange and motley crowd was interned there, babbling in many tongues and wearing the costumes of many nationalities. They gathered in the courtyard twice a day for roll call. There were Turks with baggy trousers, and their wives had veiled faces with only dark eyes showing. Arabs with flowing white garments and red fezes, white-robed priests from African colonies of France, gypsies in gay colors and dangling earrings, artists and scholars with velvet jackets and flowing ties, merchantmen in sailors' uniforms, and men in plain, somber business suits.

There were shoemakers and tailors, bankers and merchants, architects, engineers, waiters, hotel managers and artists, scholars and musicians, all caught by the war in a country that was not their own. But there was no other doctor. An old country doctor, practicing in the neighborhood, was called in whenever he was needed to look after the sick.

In the camp the days passed, each one like the other. Some of the people, in their boredom, paced the little courtyard around and around like caged animals, glancing wistfully now and then up over the high walls to the blue sky and the shimmering snow-capped mountains beyond. Others gathered in little groups to talk and argue heatedly about the war and politics, some on one side and some on the other. Still others, unaccustomed to idleness, went about in search of something to do to pass the time. They repaired the old monastery as much as possible, or, with the permission of the governor of the camp, went out to help the farmers harvest the crops. And some, unable to do more, whittled little objects out of pieces of wood.

One of the men came up to Dr. Schweitzer the day after

his arrival at the internment camp and asked if there was something he could do for him.

"I want to show my appreciation to you for curing my wife of an illness," he went on.

The doctor was puzzled at his words, for he had no recollection of ever having seen the man or his wife before.

"We met a man named Classen, from Hamburg, at one of the internment camps where we were sent," the man explained. "When my wife was sick he gave her some medicine which he said you had let him have just before he was brought here from Africa, and she made a good recovery."

Now it came back to Dr. Schweitzer's memory. Richard Classen was a timber merchant from Germany, caught by the war in French Equatorial Africa, and had been made a prisoner of war. Dr. Schweitzer had prepared some medicines for him to take with him, with full directions on each bottle, telling what they were for and how they should be used. Now he was to have his fee in something made for him at this internment camp. The thing he wanted most was a table, and some loose boards were found in the loft of the monastery to make it with.

When the table was finished, Dr. Schweitzer took up again the work on his book, this time guided by the outline he had made in French.

"The Reverence for Life includes everything that can be described as love, devotion and sympathy, whether in suffering, joy or effort."

There was time enough, not only for the writing, but for music, too. The table served as an organ, and he practiced as he had done on the boat, with his fingers on the wood surface and his feet on the floor as if foot pedals were there. And in his mind he could hear the melodies of Bach and Mendelssohn.

"Are you Albert Schweitzer, the musician?" the oldest of

a group of gypsies asked him one day in the courtyard. "The one Romain Rolland wrote about in his book, *Musicians of Today?*"

When the doctor replied that he was, the gypsies were delighted. They invited him, as a fellow musician, to join them when they gathered in the monastery loft to practice and play on their violins.

The governor of the internment camp carried out his duties not only with fairness, but with kindness and understanding as well. Since the musicians were allowed to keep their musical instruments for practice, the carpenters their tools to work with, the dentists their instruments to carry on their work when needed, it was only fair, he said, to allow the camp's only doctor to practice medicine. There were people from the African colonies, and sailors from many ports, suffering from tropical diseases. With his experience and with the medicines he had with him, Dr. Schweitzer was better able to treat them than the country doctor who had been coming.

There was an old saying in Alsace that to work is to pray. Work that winter was a blessing to Dr. Schweitzer as well as to those he cared for. As he went among the sick, or as he sat at his table writing, or memorizing music and the fingering for it, he could push back for a little while the anxieties that kept nagging at his mind. His native land was once more a battleground, and the two countries he loved were fighting again for its possession. What was happening to his own people there, he wondered. How were his parents? And his brother and sisters? What had become of his godmother Barth and his Uncle Louis and Aunt Sophie, and all the dear friends he had known at Strasbourg?

Others wanting to lose themselves in work could envy the doctor his many interests and careers. Tailors, longing to have scissors and needle in their hands again, offered to make a dress for the doctor's wife out of some material which she had, just for the pleasure of the work.

A group of men, a shoemaker, a basket weaver, a milliner, a tailor and a brush maker, wanted to take over the cooking. They could manage better than the ones now in the kitchen, though they were all former chefs, they said. The governor decided, since they were so insistent, that he would let them try, in spite of the fact that none of them had ever cooked before.

"If you succeed, you can take over the jobs as cooks," he said. "But if you fail, you'll be put under lock and key for creating a disturbance."

The men agreed that that was fair enough. They went into the kitchen and on that first day they turned out a meal of potatoes and cabbage fit for a king. From then on, each meal they served was better than the last. Everyone agreed that they were better than the real cooks, who had once worked in the fashionable restaurants of Paris. And they were kept on as cooks of the internment camp.

"How do you do it?" Dr. Schweitzer asked the leader of the group who was a shoemaker by trade. "How can you prepare such tasty meals with what you are given, and with no experience? What is your secret?"

"There are all sorts of things that one should know, of course," the shoemaker replied. "But the most important thing is to do the cooking with love and care."

Life in an internment camp was an education in itself. The doctor found himself picking up bits of information that winter he would never have had from books or from colleges and universities. Confined within the high monastery walls with men of many different nationalities and many different walks of life, he learned about such widely varying things as banking, architecture, factory building and furnace making, from experts in those fields. The gypsy musicians told of playing in French restaurants; hotel managers, tailors, merchants, talked of the work they had done.

The ones Dr. Schweitzer pitied were those who could not lose themselves in work, the restless ones. Pale, cold children of the internment camp, he called them. They had no appetite for food, as good as it was then, and they became weak and undernourished so that the slightest ailment could become something serious. He saw them pacing the courtyard day after day, or standing about the corridors if it rained too hard to be outside, listless and sick at heart. Their loyalty was torn between the country of their birth and the country where they had chosen to live. Some had married French wives, and had children who spoke no other language than French. The doctor listened while they talked over their problems, and the sympathy and understanding he gave was better than any medicine.

The winter was unusually cold that year, and it was felt even more by those who had come from the tropical heat of the Equator. But the mountain air was dry and clear, in spite of the cold, and in time the doctor and his wife began to feel restored in health.

With spring came the order that Albert and Helene Schweitzer were to be transferred to a camp at St. Rémy de Provence, where Alsatians only were sent. They found there old friends, some from their childhood and some former pupils and colleagues. The governor of this camp was friendly and fair to those in his charge, as the one was at the former camp.

"Nothing is allowed," he would often say, when he was asked if such and such a thing could be done. "But," he would add with a twinkle, "there are things that are tolerated if you are reasonable."

The cold of the winter stayed on until late, and the spring was damp and bleak, with a cold north wind blowing down from the Alps. The building at St. Rémy, with its walled-in garden, had also been a monastery taken over long ago by the government. When Dr. Schweitzer went into the big reception room on the ground floor for the first time, he had a strange feeling that he had seen this place somewhere. There was something familiar about the bare ugliness of the room, the stone floors, the iron stove with its pipe crossing from one side to the other. Yet he knew he had never been here before in his whole life.

The mystery was finally solved. He had seen the room in a drawing by the artist van Gogh. The old monastery had been used, until only recently, as a hospital for the insane, and the artist had been a patient here. He had sat in the big reception room as the doctor was doing now. And he had walked in the little garden between the high walls, and he had felt the north wind blow over the cold floors of the corridor as it still did.

Three and a half months later news came that they would all be sent back to their homes in Alsace in exchange for the same number of French prisoners of war that Germany had been holding. There was a buzz of excitement over the whole camp as everyone began to pack and make their preparations to leave. Dr. Schweitzer took his sketches for the *Philosophy of Civilization* which he had worked on at both camps and showed them to the censor. They were stamped and allowed to pass.

When the convoy was passing through the gate to take them to the railway station, Dr. Schweitzer rushed back to the governor's office to say good-by. There he found the governor, sitting dejected and alone, for he felt deeply the departure of these Alsatians who had been in his charge. "My boarders," he liked to call them.

There was no bitterness in Dr. Schweitzer's heart, as there well might have been, for the months spent in internment camps. It was something every country at war must do for its own defense, he realized. He grieved instead for those on battlefields and in trenches, suffering, or bringing suffering to others. As for himself, he had seen goodness at the bottom of men's hearts, and little kindnesses shown to friend and enemy alike. He thought of the poor cripple, a camp patient he had treated, who had helped him carry his luggage to the station. The cripple himself had few belongings of his own. And as the two men walked together in the hot July sun, the doctor made another vow. In memory of this man he would always keep on the watch for heavily laden people in railway stations where he chanced to be. He thought, too, of the French men and women who met their train at one of the little stations along the way. Thinking this was the train coming in from Germany with the French prisoners of war, they escorted the travelers to tables loaded with delicious food. When they suddenly realized their mistake, there was embarrassment at first on both sides. Then all joined in a hearty laugh and a feeling of friendship came over them.

As the train taking them out of France went on its way, it grew longer and longer, with coaches added from other camps. Two were filled with basket weavers and kettle menders, scissors grinders, tramps and gypsies, also being exchanged.

They went a short distance through neutral Switzerland, with its neat, green farms and vineyards and its tidy houses. Then they crossed the border into Alsace. It was like coming to another planet. There the people were thin and pale, and had a look of utter weariness. And at night the streets were dark, with not a glimmer of light shining from the houses.

Since Günsbach was close to the firing line, Dr. Schweitzer had to apply for permission at Strasbourg to be allowed to go there. Even after it was given, he could only go as far as Colmar on the train. The last ten miles he had to walk, between lines of wire fencing packed with straw. There were brick emplacements for machine guns everywhere he turned, and one after another of the houses he passed had been ruined by gunfire. The hills he had once loved with their wooded patches on the slopes were bare now, except for a few stumps left here and there. The dull roar of cannons could be heard from the crest, and in the villages along the way there were signs posted warning everyone to carry a gasmask about with him.

This was the smiling, peaceful valley he had left more than five years ago on that Good Friday when the church bells were ringing.

At Günsbach he had to make his way through crowds of soldiers, and past lines of battered houses, until he came to the manse. The place had been taken over by soldiers quartered there, but his father had stayed on in spite of it. His mother had been killed, run over by the horses of soldiers passing through.

There followed a period of sickness for the doctor that not even the good air of his native Alsace could cure. He had a feeling of languor, then pain and high fever. It was comforting to be with his father again, seeing him in the old familiar study, with the lamp's soft glow shining on his gentle face. There was a restful calmness about him. Even during a bombardment, when others in the village rushed to their cellars, he remained where he was.

Helene Schweitzer was finally allowed to join her husband at Günsbach, but even with these two he loved he did not recover until he returned to Strasbourg for surgery.

"The Fellowship of Those Who Bear the Mark of Pain." He who had been so healthy from the time he was a small boy knew now from experience what physical pain and bodily anguish meant. Such men belonged together the world over, he felt. They were united by a common experience.

He remembered the sick and the suffering he had seen in Africa. A restlessness came over him, but he dared not think about his return. There was no way of knowing when, if ever, that would be. It seemed to him that he was like a coin that had rolled under a piece of furniture and remained there, lost.

The war came to an end on the eleventh of November of that year of 1918. Alsace now belonged to France, and Dr. Schweitzer became by that treaty a French citizen, as his parents had also been before the German victory of 1870.

When he had recovered enough to take up his work again, Dr. Schweitzer was offered a position at the Municipal Hospital in Strasbourg. He was also given his old post as curate at the little Church of St. Nicholas. His two former associates had been removed, one by the Germans during the war because he was pro-French, and the other by the French after the war because he was pro-German.

It was good to be working again, healing the sick and conducting services at the little church he had been so fond of. And now he could begin to pay back the debts he had incurred to carry on his hospital during those last years in Africa.

This burden of debts had been weighing heavily on his mind. He had borrowed from the Paris Missionary Society and from kind friends in France, and it would take him a long time to pay it all back, but now he could at least make the start. He dared not plan beyond that.

Once more the people of Alsace set to work to clear away the debris brought by the war. They repaired the damage done to their houses, plowed their fields and planted their vineyards again. But in Germany, crushed in defeat, there was hunger and despair. During the armistice period and for two years afterward, the doctor was a familiar figure to the customs officials as he crossed the border with his knapsack full of food for Cosima, the widow of Richard Wagner, and for an aged painter, Hans Thoma, and his sister.

A letter came one day from Sweden inviting Dr. Schweitzer to come to the University at Upsala and give a series of lectures. He went there, tired and depressed, still feeling the effects of his recent illness. But after a few weeks his health was entirely restored. His old enthusiasm for his work came back. The Archbishop who had invited him there took him into his own home as his guest, and arranged other lectures throughout Sweden when his talks at the University were over. A young Swedish student interpreted for him, translating sentence by sentence in such a lively way that the audience could feel they were understanding the original words instead of the translation.

There were organ recitals during that visit also. It was a joy to play the old Swedish organs, with their resonance suited to his way of playing Bach.

When the visit was over, the doctor returned to Strasbourg with enough money earned to pay off the most pressing of his debts. Now, with his good health restored, he could begin to look toward the future. He made up his mind that he would return to Lambaréné, and take up again the work he had started there.

It was not the same as when he had decided the first time that he would go. He knew what lay ahead of him. It was not an easy life he was choosing, and there would be times of discouragement. But there would be his reward also, in seeing the sick made well again.

Dr. Schweitzer gave up his work at Strasbourg and moved with his wife, and the little daughter born on his birthday, January 14, to live with his father in the manse at Günsbach. There he spent his time writing, trying to finish the work he had started before leaving for Africa.

Five books were published within three years during that

period. The first was a book he called *On the Edge of the Primeval Forest*, which told of his experiences in Africa. It was illustrated with the photographs of Richard Classen, the timber man from Hamburg to whom he had given the medicines when he was taken as prisoner of war.

After that there were two volumes of his *Philosophy of Civilization*. The manuscript he had left for safe-keeping with the American, Mr. Ford, had reached him finally, and he put it in order, including in it the work he had done in the internment camps. The next year the book *Christianity and the Religions of the World*, taken from lectures he had given in England, was published. And at the same time, his book *Memories of Childhood and Youth* appeared.

His fame had by now spread over all of Europe and to America. His books were translated in many languages, and there were invitations to give lectures or organ recitals in Spain, Switzerland, Denmark, Czechoslovakia, Sweden, England and his native Alsace.

It was not easy to turn away in the midst of this, to leave his native soil again. And to make it worse, it was decided his wife would not join him just yet. The climate of the tropics had been too trying for her, and she dared not go with a small child.

It was with sadness that the doctor said good-by to them and to his father. But he could not do otherwise than go. He felt it was only a matter of course that he should take his share of the burden of pain which lay upon the world. Each must go his own way. He would return from time to time, and his wife made plans to join him in Africa, as often as she was able.

A young Oxford student went with the doctor to spend a few months helping him get started with his work again.

Chapter XI

The one essential thing is that we strive to have light in ourselves. Our strivings will be recognized by others, and when people have light in themselves, it will shine out from them. Then we get to know each other as we walk together in the darkness.

Memoirs of Childhood and Youth

THE JOURNEY from Europe to Africa was made by cargo boat, and it took over seven weeks from the coast of France to the mouth of the Ogowe. Cape Lopez was far different now from the almost deserted village Dr. Schweitzer had known during the war years. The waterfront was crowded, and timber ships were being loaded with mahogany, ebony and okoume. Even the name of the place had been changed. It was now called Port Gentil.

There were shouts of welcome from the native workers who recognized their doctor, Oganga. Oyembo was there. He had a fine raft of okoume logs which he and some of the men from his native village had brought down to the river to sell.

"You've come far, Oyembo," the doctor said, as he shook hands with his old friend and interpreter. "Now that you're in the timber business, you're well on your way to becoming a rich man."

"I can't complain," Oyembo answered.

The doctor was on the point of asking about his wife and children when Oyembo had to rush away to see about the delivery of his timber. Dr. Schweitzer then went back to attend to his own baggage as it went through the customs.

Among the many boxes and trunks, there were four potato sacks filled with letters which he had not had time to answer before leaving Europe. The customs officer who had examined his baggage, before it left the port of France, had been puzzled at finding so many letters unopened and all addressed to one man. He was sure there was some trick in it. Smuggled gold, perhaps, which the government of France had forbidden to be taken out of the country. For an hour and a half the poor customs official had gone through the letters, opening them one by one, until he reached the bottom of the second sack. Then he shook his head in bewilderment and gave it up. Four potato sacks of letters from people saying they had enjoyed a certain organ recital, or heard a certain lecture that had meant much to them, or had read a certain book which they liked very much.

The river boat, waiting to take the passengers up the Ogowe, was the same one the doctor and his wife had traveled on when they first came to this country. But what a dirty, ramshackle old boat it had become in the eleven years that had passed, the doctor thought. It was not until the boat rounded the bend that hid the port from sight that he came to the Africa he had known before. Here time had stood still. There were the same swamps with roots of trees like huge spider legs standing in the water, the same papyrus islands, with the tall, feathery stalks swaying in the breeze. From the taller trees along the banks, monkeys looked down at them with the same excited curiosity. There were also the tumble-down villages he had known, with inhabitants as ragged and poor as ever.

Among the passengers on the boat there were many acquaintances he had known before, timber merchants and government officials. They gave the doctor a hearty welcome, and they told of all that had happened during the time he had been away.

That night, after dinner was over, Dr. Schweitzer went out on deck alone. Water birds skimmed in and out among the pale reeds, singing their sleepy evening songs. The green banks darkened slowly, then the full Easter moon rose above the treetops. Its soft silver light gave an enchanting beauty to the river and the forest in the distance. He was truly in Africa now, Africa with all her misery and her loveliness.

The boat reached Lambaréné at sunrise on the day before Easter. The canoes from the mission station were waiting to take the doctor and his young assistant, Noel, with all their crates and boxes and trunks, on up the river to the hospital.

After an hour of paddling, the canoes rounded the bend of the island and entered the side channel. The doctor looked eagerly toward the three small hills for a glimpse of the buildings of the mission station. How long it had been since he had seen them last, and how much had happened in the years between. He had often given up hope of ever seeing them again. Now he could scarcely believe he was here at last. There was only one thing that marred the joy of coming back. His wife and child were not here to share it with him.

Noel, the young English student, stayed at the landing to look after the unloading of the canoes, but Dr. Schweitzer was impatient to see the old hospital again. He walked up the slope like one in a dream. It was like coming up on the hidden castle of Sleeping Beauty. Tangled weeds and shrubs were growing where there were once log buildings which had been built with so much care. Nothing was left but the two buildings of corrugated iron with cement floors, and they were half covered by branches of tall trees that had been only saplings when Dr. Schweitzer had seen them last. Their roofs, thatched with raffia, were falling apart so that even they were not habitable. One room was still in fair condition, and for that the doctor was grateful, for it was the place where he had stored his medical supplies in their strong wooden boxes, seven years ago.

The group of missionaries who had welcomed him at the river landing caught up with him and joined him as he started on toward his old cottage on the crest of the hill. They had done the best they could to keep the buildings in repair, but they had had to give it up for lack of labor and material. Now that there was such a demand for timber in Europe and America, anyone who could handle an ax found well-paid work in the forest. And anyone who knew about timber rafts found a job floating them down the river. Everyone was so busy that no time was left for the slow job of making roof tiles of raffia palm leaves and stitching them to bamboo poles to thatch the houses.

"The first thing tomorrow morning, I'll have the boys of the mission clear this path for you," one of the missionaries said, as they made their way through the tall weeds and undergrowth.

"Never mind," the doctor said. "Let me trample it down with my own footsteps."

He lost no time in starting. During that very afternoon he and Noel set out in a canoe in search of leaf roof tiles in the neighboring villages. The sick would be arriving, as soon as word was spread that the doctor had returned. Now that the rainy season was on, there would have to be a dry place to treat the patients, and a ward to house those who needed to stay on. Room must be found also to unpack the medical supplies that had been left here, as well as the seventy-two packing cases he had sent from Europe, which were due any time.

New tribes had moved in to settle on the Ogowe River since the doctor had been here last, and more were constantly coming to join them. They were the Bendjabis, and they came from deep in the jungle, half starved, half naked, bringing their miserable little belongings on their heads. Short of stature, with the faces of true savages, scarred with tribal marks, they were looked down upon by the Galoas, whose people had belonged to this region. They were even despised by the Pahouins, whom the Galoas thought of as inferior.

When the work in the hospital was started, these people came bringing their sick after their own witch doctors had failed to cure. Often they were the cause of trouble, since not only were the white man's ways different from their own, but their jungle customs were different from those of the river people, as well.

Sometimes the doctor asked for help in carrying a sick man on a stretcher, or in giving support to one with a wounded leg. More often than not, the answer was, "No. That person is not of my tribe."

The doctor's patience was exhausted many times with the Bendjabis, for their lack of regard for the property rights of others. They took what they wanted, no matter whose it was or what it was. Even the food was stolen from a patient too sick to prevent it. They showed no sign of gratitude, and the relatives who came with them sat with sullen faces, refusing to show any indication of friendliness.

If only he could sit around a fire and talk as man to man with his patients, Dr. Schweitzer often thought. If he could be looked upon as something more than a medicine man and a custodian of hospital law and order, there would be a better understanding between them. But his whole time was taken up now with carrying on the struggle against sickness and pain, and with the physical labor of repairing the buildings to treat and house the patients.

He sometimes came across some former patient when one of his journeys to visit the sick took him near a timber site. And the face which he had thought sullen at the hospital beamed with pleasure at seeing him. Again a Bendjabi paddler, passing close to the hospital in his canoe, would call out a hearty greeting to the doctor, though he might not have spoken one civil word during his whole time as a patient. One needed to look deeply to know the true nature of these people.

Dr. Schweitzer saw a look of horror come over the face of one man brought from the interior for an emergency operation. When he was put on the operating table, his expression plainly showed that he believed he had fallen among cannibals. No one could speak his language, and the doctor's soothing words could not be interpreted for him. For all he could understand, they might have been the incantation a witch doctor or a leopard man would use. The anesthetic put an end to his terror. And when he woke again, free from his torturing pain, a smile came over his face that expressed his gratitude and understanding more than any spoken word.

Joseph returned to take up his old work at the hospital as soon as he learned that the doctor was back. He had at last, in the past seven years, saved enough from wages earned in a timber camp, to buy a wife. Now he had ambitions to become a timber trader on his own. He and some friends had rented a large area of forest, three days' journey away, which meant he would have to take a leave of absence from the hospital whenever he was needed at the timber site.

Aloys, the cook, came back also. But there was no word from Oyembo, the teacher. He was the one whom the doctor missed most of all. He had had such high hopes for Oyembo. Such a man as that, intelligent, noble, upright, could do much for his people, not only through leadership but by example as well. Africa needed help from her own native sons more even than from strangers.

It was with a sad heart that the doctor passed the little house near the boys' school, where Oyembo and his family had once lived. He could not bring himself to talk about

Oyembo, even with the others at the mission station, or to ask news of him.

There was no dry season the first year of the doctor's return. The rains that should have ended in May kept on all through the summer months. It was something no one had ever experienced before. Something they had never heard the old folks say had happened in other years. They couldn't understand it. There were no words in their language for winter or summer, and the missionaries had translated the promise God made to Noah after the Flood: While the earth remainest, wet season and dry season, day and night, shall not cease.

"If that is what God promised, then why is it the weather does not go on as the Bible says it will?" the people wanted to know.

What answer could he give, the doctor wondered. He worried about a coming famine and the sickness that always follows. From May to August was the season when the land should be cleared, all trees and undergrowth cut down and burned so that new land, made rich by wood ash, could be used for the banana plantations. It was bad enough that so many men had left the villages to work at timber camps, where the wages were spent as quickly as they were earned. But now, with the rainstorms coming one after the other, those who had stayed on in their villages had no heart for clearing land, when nothing would dry out enough to burn.

The Father Superior of the Catholic Mission across the channel went out with twelve of the boys from the school on a hippopotamus hunt, to be gone for two weeks. Only if they came back with a canoe-load of smoked hippopotamus meat could the school go on. If they returned empty-handed, the school would have to close.

Dr. Schweitzer began buying rice to keep in reserve, for whatever else might happen his patients must be fed.

August came, and it was time for the young student Noel to return to England and take up his studies at Oxford. He had been four months in Africa, and not only had he been a medical assistant, giving injections and medicines, but he had been foreman, carpenter, typist and sexton as well. The "doctor's lieutenant," the Africans called him, for the war years had made them familiar with army terms. They were as sorry as the doctor himself to see the youth go.

A nurse, Mlle. Mathilda Kottman, came out from Alsace, and a young doctor, Victor Nessmann, also joined the staff, for the work had increased and was too much for one doctor to handle.

"Now you can rest, for I'll take over all the work," the young doctor said, as soon as he stepped off the boat at Lambaréné.

Dr. Schweitzer smiled at his words. This youth, the son of one of his fellow students at Strasbourg, had the health and boundless energy he himself had had at that age.

"Good," the doctor answered. "You can begin now by looking after the loading of your trunks and cases in the canoes."

Dr. Nessmann proved to be a good stevedore. And as time passed, he showed that he was the type of young man made for the work in Africa. He was practical, he had the Alsatian gift for organization and he could get along well with the people. Most important of all, he had a sense of humor that would see him through periods of disappointment and discouragement that a doctor must expect.

"The Little Doctor," he was called by the natives, though he towered above them all, and was even taller than Dr. Schweitzer himself. Dr. Schweitzer was always referred to as the "Grand Doctor."

Not only was there the added help of these two young Alsatians, but some of the Africans had learned to do work as orderlies in the hospital. Joseph could now give intravenous injections, as well as bandage wounds. But in spite of young Dr. Nessmann's prediction, there was little rest for Dr. Schweitzer.

The sick came crowding in so that both doctors were kept constantly busy. The lepers came, and the victims of the tsetse fly, suffering from sleeping sickness, and the victims, too, of the mosquito that carried malaria. Many came hobbling up with sores covering their feet and legs. The old came, looking for a last home, and orphan babies were brought in to be fed. Some came who had been poisoned by an enemy, and some who had been attacked by an elephant or wild buffalo.

One man had been wounded by a leopard while he lay sleeping in his hut. The animal had seized the man's right arm, but had let it go when the man's neighbors had come rushing in with torches. It took twelve hours by canoe to reach the hospital with the wounded man. Only four tiny pricks showed in the swollen skin, where the claws had broken through, but underneath, the flesh was torn to the bone, and high fever had set in. He was treated at once, and was soon well enough to return to his village.

Another man was bitten by a gorilla. And still another had been tossed in the air and gored by an elephant. And there were some brought in with wounds from human bites.

"The worst bite is a leopard's bite," Joseph said. "Worse than that is the bite of a poisonous snake. Still worse is a monkey's bite. But the very worst bite of all is the bite of a man."

The hospital became a refuge of safety, not only for the sick and the old and the orphan babies, but for the insane, and the lepers. Many came there also, seeking escape from some revenge.

One morning a man brought in a companion he had shot by

mistake, thinking he was a wild boar in the underbrush. The wound was fatal, and as soon as the victim died the unhappy hunter sent at once for his wife and child to join him at the hospital. Dr. Schweitzer went with him to the office of the District Commissioner, so the case could be tried within the law instead of letting the victim's family take their revenge. The man was sentenced to pay a certain sum of money to the victim's family, and because according to the law of the jungle a life must be given for a life, he was sentenced to give a goat as well to the survivors. The doctor allowed him to stay on at the hospital with his family and work until he had earned enough money for the fine.

The famine had become serious. Since the continuous rains in the summer of 1924 had kept the people from clearing their forest patches and burning the brush, they could do no planting that year. They might have cut up the timber in small pieces and hauled it away, or piled it up so there would be room enough between the piles for banana trees and manioc. But that was not the way they had been used to planting, and they would do it only the way they had always done. They resigned themselves to their fate, and sat in their villages waiting for death. An evil spell had been cast on the earth, they believed, and there was nothing they could do to break it.

How badly these people needed some leader among them, one of their own kind to raise them out of the bondage of their superstitions and fears and ignorance.

"I came across Oyembo, our old schoolteacher, not long ago," one of the missionaries said to Dr. Schweitzer one day.

"Oh yes, Oyembo," the doctor replied. "There's another one lost in the commerce of wood who might have been a help to his people. He, of all the others, I had had the most hope for."

"Lost! What are you talking about?" the missionary exclaimed in surprise.

The doctor told of seeing Oyembo at the wharf of Port Gentil, when he had arrived from Europe.

"He's a successful businessman now, and no longer the teacher of his people as we knew him here."

"A businessman, yes," the missionary answered. "But he hasn't given up teaching. The work he's doing now in education is far more important than what he was doing here when you knew him."

The missionary went on to tell of how, during the war, Oyembo had returned to his little village in the brush. There he talked to the people, and persuaded them to go out with him and clear a large section of the forest for a plantation. Like those in other villages of Africa, they had never cleared more than barely enough land to supply food to satisfy their hunger. But Oyembo wanted a place large enough to feed the whole village, with enough left over to sell to the timber men for their workers. They planted bananas and manioc for their staple diet, and also coffee and cacao to take to the market.

He also started a school in his village, without asking help from either the government or the missions, and he took the time out to teach it himself. The children helped work in the plantation for money for their books, and it gave them a feeling of pride and independence.

Oyembo was not content with teaching the children only. He wanted to bring a new way of life to the whole village. Until that time the people had built miserable little huts of bamboo and mud that scarcely held together enough to shelter them from the sun and rain. Now they were shown how to build with more skill, and within a few months after Oyembo's return his village had the largest, sturdiest houses of any in that part of Africa. He called upon the men to help him clear the underbrush that grew up to the edge of the village, for he had learned that it was a breeding place for malaria-bearing mosquitoes and tsetse flies. They cleared the land up to the lake, which let the cool evening breezes blow in freely.

After the war was over, and the timber trade commenced again, Oyembo led the men out into the forest and taught them how to work together in harmony. He kept a record of how much was spent and how much received and the hours of labor each man put in. And the people learned that by their own labors they could better their condition.

It had not been easy. Many of the men rebelled at working more than was absolutely necessary. Who was this Oyembo, coming back with ways he had learned from the whites and telling them what to do, they wanted to know. But Oyembo won them over, not so much by eloquent speeches as by example and the goodness of his own character.

It was not long after the doctor heard this news of his old friend that Oyembo came to the hospital to pay him a call. Dr. Schweitzer told him then of how he had rejoiced when he heard of the good he had done in his village. But Oyembo, ever modest, would say little about his own part in it. If only there were one such man in every village, what a magnificent country Africa could become, the doctor thought.

So many of the patients in the hospital were there because they were victims of their own superstition, ignorance and lack of cleanliness or effort.

The hospital was constantly crowded. There was more work than two doctors could possibly do. And another nurse was needed. Young Dr. Lauterburg of Switzerland and Mlle. Emma Hausknecht of Alsace answered the call and came to devote themselves to helping the unfortunates in this land far from their homes.

The famine continued into the following year. There was no food but rice, and even that was becoming scarce and hard to find. Work at many of the timber camps had come to a standstill. What would happen if the hospital, too, should have to be abandoned, the doctor wondered. How could he turn the sick away and send them back to their famine-stricken villages? Many had come from as far as sixty or ninety miles away. Even in ordinary times it was often a problem to discharge the cured and their relatives promptly. Those from far off had to wait until a canoe or motorboat happened to be going their way. Now it was worse, for the people stayed on as long as possible, dreading to go back to the hunger awaiting them in their villages. But it always seemed to happen that just as the supply of rice for the hospital was running short and there was despair of getting any more, something would turn up. Those who had managed to find sacks of rice they could buy shared with others less fortunate. Often one timber merchant gave part of his supplies to a rival who had none. And at the hospital, where at least a hundred and seventy-five pounds a day were needed, the doctor sent some to a mission station up the river that was in need, and he gave to merchants and to an English factory in the region.

The famine taught Dr. Schweitzer one valuable lesson. The hospital must have its own plantation to assure a food supply in spite of whatever famines there might be in the future. But where would it be? The little hill where the hospital stood afforded scarcely room for the buildings that had been repaired or put up since his return to Africa. It had been planned for no more than fifty patients and there were now three times that many. Suppose a fire should break out! The doctor shuddered at the thought, for, huddled close together as they were, one small flame could destroy all the buildings at once. More room was badly needed, room for a large plantation of bananas and one of manioc. And there ought to be a garden of vegetables such as were grown in Europe and America, and also an orchard where there could be orange and grapefruit trees. There ought to be tropical fruit in such abundance that the patients and their families could have all they wanted. And there ought to be room for the hospital to grow, with more buildings added as they were needed.

There was a place not two miles up the river from the mission station that the doctor had often noticed. It was the site of an old Galoa village, where the chief of the tribe, N'Kombe, the Sun King, had lived. The natives called the place Adolinanongo, which meant in their language, "That which looks out over all the tribes." It was well named, for it was there that the river divided into two branches, and there was a magnificent view of sky and water and green forests, with the low blue hills on the horizon. And the little villages in the clearings, dotted here and there along the shore, could be clearly seen.

A plan began to form in the doctor's mind. He went again to the place and walked alone up the gently rising slope. In his imagination he could see the forest cleared away, and well-built, spacious buildings surrounded by fruit trees and plantations.

Chapter XII

The power of ideals is incalculable. We see no power in a drop
of water. But let it get into a crack in the rock and be turned to
ice, and it splits the rock; turned into steam, it drives the pistons
of the most powerful engines. Something has happened to it which
makes active and effective the power hidden in it.

Memoirs of Childhood and Youth

ONE EVENING after his return from a mysterious journey
away from the hospital, Dr. Schweitzer called the two doctors and the two nurses together, saying that he had some
news for them. He told how the hospital would be moved
to a larger site, and explained that he had waited until he was
sure of his plans before mentioning them. But now the District Commissioner had agreed to let the hospital have the
use of the tract of land, a hundred and seventy-two acres, on
the site of the old Galoa village.

At first his co-workers were speechless with surprise. Then
they broke into shouts of joy, and all began talking at once.
They made their plans then and there. There would be
stronger buildings, space for isolation wards, space to spread
out and grow, space to plant food for the sick and for themselves. But what an undertaking it would be! The place had
gone back to jungle completely in the years since it had been
abandoned.

The Africans standing near stared in astonishment. Never
had they seen such gesticulations, or heard such chatter from
these Europeans. It was like one of their own palavers when
the men met and talked under the roof of their palaver houses.

The first thing to be done was to stake out the area granted to them so that the ground plan could be made and shown to the District Commissioner for his approval. Compass in hand, Dr. Schweitzer worked his way through the tangled forest, with his helpers following close behind. Up on the high ground they made blazes on the trees, and in the swamps they drove long poles into the soft earth, about sixty feet apart. After that the work of clearing was begun.

Dr. Schweitzer could compare a day with these men to the movements of a symphony. Lento—they start off slowly, with reluctance. Moderato—axes and bush knives move with extreme moderation which the conductor tries in vain to quicken. Noon and the rest period put an end to the movement. Adagio—the people go back to work after much persuasion. Not a breath of wind stirs. The sound of an ax is heard from time to time. Scherzo—a few jokes from the doctor; now laughter and merry words. A few begin to sing. A breath of wind blows up from the river. Finale—Now everyone is lively. Howling and yelling, they attack the trees. Axes and bush knives fly louder and faster until at last the doctor shouts *Amani! Amani!* Enough. The work is ended for the day.

The workers still chattered as they collected their tools and put them back in the canoes for the return trip down the river. What a strange person the Grand Doctor was! He'd pick up a lizard or a frog and put it out of harm's way when he was helping with the digging or the clearing. And not only did he want to spare animals, but there were trees he spared as well. A kapok tree, yes. That they could understand. It was the tree of the chiefs. Every village had a kapok tree where the old men gathered and told tales of other days, when animals could talk with men. The kapok was a magic tree, with leaves that made good medicine to cure any sickness. But the Grand Doctor made them spare not only the kapok tree, but oil palms as well. The way they had to tunnel through the creepers to get to a scraggly little palm and clear around it, when the easiest thing would have been to cut everything in sight and let it dry, then burn the whole forest. Think of the animals they might have trapped that way. Enough to supply them with meat for many a day. Oh well, the doctor would never stand for such a thing in any case.

They pushed aside the blossoming lantanas and the broad elephant ear plants and they stepped through ferns and wild cannas growing as tall as a man.

Look up to the high branches! Make sure there's no python overhead. Watch out for adders lurking at your feet. Listen closely for the sound of leopards or gorillas hidden in the brush. Don't step near a line of driver ants. Take care the tsetse flies and mosquitoes don't bite. Nettles sting your feet, and jiggers get in your toes.

"Tsa! tsa! N'goumka tsa!"

They sang a song about the jiggers.

"A man can't dance when he has jiggers in his toes."

But it was no laughing matter. Scarcely a grown-up native in the region had all ten of his toes, because of this tiny insect that burrowed under the nail and caused serious infection.

As the work went on, the doctor could see the dream take shape that he had cherished for a long time. Some day the place would be a Garden of Eden with hundreds of fruit trees started from seeds. He would have every kind of fruit and vegetable that could be grown in a tropical climate. Here in this land where nature had provided no edible plant, where everything that bore fruit or leaf or root for food had been brought here and transplanted, there would now be food for all. There would be oil to cook it in from the oil palms left standing. And a herd of goats would be brought in, bred to resist the tsetse fly, so there would be milk for the sick and the orphan babies. Perhaps there would even be a time when food would be so plentiful that everyone could take all he wanted, and there would be no more hunger and famine, and no crime of stealing to eat.

Slowly the hospital buildings themselves began to take shape. There was much that the doctor had learned in the years since he had first come to the tropics, and it was well he had this experience behind him before starting to build a permanent hospital. There would be no more bamboo buildings with leaf roofs, such as were used throughout this part of Africa. They were constantly in need of repair to keep them from falling apart. This meant that the doctors themselves must take valuable time from their care of the sick, to turn carpenter and handyman. Stone or brick were out of the question. Either would take too much time or money. Corrugated iron on a stout framework of wood was the only solution, and it should be painted to deflect the rays of the sun.

Close to the Equator the sun veers little from north to south. Winter and summer its course is directly overhead. The buildings then must be long and narrow, with the gabled ends facing east and west to bear the slanting rays of the sun. And the whole length along the north and south sides could be opened to the breeze.

Five buildings were planned, enough for more than two hundred patients and the relatives or friends who came with them. They were built on the slope of the hill, where the sick could look out on the Ogowe River and see their canoes, tied at the landing, waiting to take them back to their villages when they were well.

In the midst of all this work, the news reached Dr. Schweitzer that the University of Prague had conferred on him an honorary degree. How far away that kind of world was from this jungle of giant trees and savage vines and creepers and wild animals lurking in the brush. At times it seemed as if it were another planet, those hushed crowds in the dimly lit auditorium, listening as he spoke to them from the platform or as he played the organ. And yet these two worlds were closely interwoven, forming the warp and woof of one pattern. The people in the audience, who had listened and applauded in appreciation, and the ones who read his books, were the ones who wrote the letters that were still coming in by the sackload with each mail. With their words of encouragement and their contributions, they were all a part of this work in the primeval forest. Because of them it was now possible to build the kind of hospital Dr. Schweitzer needed.

It was this that convinced him more than ever that within the hearts of most men there were hidden forces of goodness. Many, he knew, were willing and eager to devote their lives to relieving the suffering and misery of their fellow men. When it was impossible to take an active part in this kind of work, they helped and shared with him. The good of these people, the many who had with their contributions helped him to carry on, might be unseen and unknown by all but a few. But it was there, a thousand times greater than the good that attracts the attention of the world. He could compare it as the deep sea might be compared to the waves that stir the surface. He looked upon himself as the deputy of those who made it possible for him to work here, and the thought made him feel humble.

When enough of the buildings were finished, the patients were moved. All day the doctor spent on the river with the patients in the canoes, going from the old hospital to the new. That evening when he took his usual tour to see that all was well, he was greeted from behind the mosquito net of every bed, and from all the relatives gathered around their cooking pots.

"It's a good hut, Doctor. A very good hut."

For the first time in their lives these people were housed as human beings should be housed, under tight, weatherproofed roofs, with floors of cement instead of the bare earth.

Two more European doctors came out to join in the work, and there were nurses added to the staff as well. Now it was possible to reach the sick who lived far away and were not able to stand the trying journey to the hospital. There was always one of the doctors who could be spared to go out with necessary medicines and instruments and treat the patients in their own villages.

Joseph left the hospital about the time the new buildings were completed. His experience as a timber merchant had not been successful, and he went off to work in a timber camp as a laborer. When he and the doctor parted it was with a touch of sadness for both at the thought of bringing an end to the association that had lasted since the hospital's beginning. Even in his new work of cutting timber, Joseph still called himself Dr. Schweitzer's "First Assistant." And he delighted to explain to awed listeners in the brush how he had given injections with the hypodermic needle.

When the hospital on the new site was running smoothly, Dr. Schweitzer could begin to think about a well-earned leave of absence, to be with his family again in Alsace. He could leave this time, secure in the knowledge that there were capable hands to take over the work while he was away.

"Doctor, have you given orders that nobody can send me away while you're gone?" a man said, running up to the doctor when he heard the news that he was leaving.

He was one of the mental patients who had been brought in a few months earlier, bound in chains, for in his mental darkness he had killed a woman of his tribe. Now he was restored enough to walk about the grounds, and could even help with light work such as sharpening axes. Here at the hospital he was quiet and contented, except for the nagging fear that he might be sent back to his village and the fate that awaited him there.

"Of course, N'Tschambi," the doctor answered. "No one can send you away without first having a long palaver with me."

The man pressed both the doctor's hands, with tears of relief streaming down his brown cheeks.

Six months after the move to the new hospital was made, Dr. Schweitzer stood on deck of the steamer that was taking him back to Europe. The ship pushed slowly out of the bay in the bright sunshine, and slowly the low, palm-fringed coastline receded in the distance. With that pain he always felt at leaving a place he loved, he stood watching the Ogowe and all its interweaving branches fade into this green strip of coastline, until it disappeared from view. And with it, the savage mystery and cruelty of Africa faded, with only its beauty remaining in the memory.

How fond one could become of the people here, in spite of the trouble they sometimes gave, the doctor thought. Once he had had to remind Dr. Nessmann, the Little Doctor, when he had been impatient and annoyed over some trying experience with the Bendjabis.

"You'll look back some day upon these same people with affection and regret at leaving them."

When there was nothing to see from the deck but water on all sides, Dr. Schweitzer went below to stow away his belongings in the cabin. This would deaden a little the pain that parting gave to him.

Among his fellow passengers were timber merchants and missionaries from the Ogowe region. They, too, were returning for a leave to be with their families in Europe, for Africa at that time was not a safe place for small children, or for those who could not stand the trying climate.

The doctor joined the men as they sat together talking of

the country they were leaving, and its people. Some felt a nostalgia for the place already, and others, who had been there too long, were critical. One, a timber buyer, complained about how he had paid out advances for logs that were never delivered. Another told of men selling the same rafts of logs to several buyers, collecting advance payments from each one. And they spoke of how often, when the logs were delivered, they were of poor quality and not the ones agreed upon.

"Just the same, the natives are not all like that," one of the buyers, silent until then, spoke up. "I know one you could have absolutely confidence in. He lives in the region of Alombie Lake. If you make a bargain with him, you can be sure of receiving the wood, and the quality you agreed upon. What's more, instead of demanding more and more of an advance, this man won't even accept what's offered. He'll tell you he'd rather not take any money until the delivery is made."

"That man's name is Oyembo, isn't it?" a missionary in the group asked.

"Yes, as a matter of fact, that is his name," the timber buyer answered.

The doctor listened proudly as others joined in, telling of their experiences.

"I have a story to tell about this Oyembo," still another man began. "I was on the lake once in a shallow canoe when a storm came up. The wind was against us, and we began to lose hope of ever reaching the bank. It was simply a question of how long it would be before we turned over, with the canoe filling up with water. My men were all from the interior and not one could swim.

"I didn't even dare to hope for help from the village on the bank. Only a big canoe, the kind they used to make in the old days, could have survived that storm, but no one makes them any more. And who could blame the people for not wanting to risk their own lives in a shallow boat like our own, trying to save us?

"Suddenly I saw, coming toward us in the storm, just such a large boat as they had long ago. It reached us as we commenced to list and overturn. The men in the boat not only reached out a hand to take us in, but they saved my baggage as well. They took us to the village where our clothes were dried, and where we were well housed and fed. The chief invited me to his own home, where he had my baggage opened so everything could dry out. The next morning when I repacked, not a thing was missing. That's not all, when I said good-by and thanked the chief, I asked what I owed the men of his village for all they had done.

" 'Nothing,' the chief replied. 'The men were only doing their duty. Good men ask nothing in exchange for that.'

"So there! That was my experience with Oyembo."

Dr. Schweitzer could think of many others among his African friends who could compare with Oyembo. Even the men the timber buyers had found fault with had some beautiful traits of character, he felt, which could be discovered if one would look beyond the difference in the code of morals and customs, and see the real man beneath. All people show themselves to one with love and patience enough to understand.

Chapter XIII

The deepest thinking is humble. It is only concerned that the flame of truth which it keeps alive should burn with the strongest and purest heat; it does not trouble about the distance to which its brightness penetrates.

Indian Thought and Its Development

FOR DR. SCHWEITZER there would always be two places, from this time on, which he would call home. And for the rest of his life there would be a tug at his heart between the two, with a reluctance to leave one and a yearning to go back to the other.

He went to a mountain resort in the Black Forest with his wife and their daughter Rhena, now five. She was old enough to listen, fascinated, to the stories he told of the wild animals at the hospital. Some had been brought in, wounded by a hunter's gun, and some had been orphaned when the mother was killed. There were the antelopes, Theckla the wild boar, Fifi the chimpanzee, a baboon, a pelican that flew in of its own accord every night to roost on the rafters outside the doctor's door. And there was the baby gorilla that was learning his table manners, eating his porridge with a spoon and wearing his bib properly. There were also two mischievous monkeys, Canada and Upsi, who played together, dashing up and down the mango trees and palms so fast one would think the trees were full of monkeys.

But Rhena must wait until she was older before she could see the animals for herself. Like all the other children of those whose work took them to Africa at that time, she must stay on in the healthier climate of Europe.

Two busy years passed. The doctor was asked to lecture or give organ recitals in Sweden, Denmark, Holland, Switzerland, England, Germany, and in the newly created country, Czechoslovakia. And in between, at every chance he had, he returned to his family, sometimes in the Black Forest and sometimes in Alsace.

Helene Schweitzer's health had improved so that she was able to go back to Africa with her husband, and little Rhena was left in the care of relatives. But after only a few months, the climate began again to tell upon Mrs. Schweitzer so that she had to leave. The doctor joined her during the following year.

There was a larger staff of doctors and nurses at the hospital now. Five doctors and as many nurses helped in the work, and though there was still much to be done, it was no longer beyond the powers of anyone to do it. And when Dr. Schweitzer took his trips to Europe every other year, he knew that the work at the hospital was being done as he had wanted it.

In 1932 he gave an address in Frankfort, Germany, at the celebration of the hundredth anniversary of Goethe's death. Here, in the crowded opera house, the doctor began his speech at the exact hour the great poet had died, on the 22nd of March. The audience listened spellbound as he addressed them, aware of the tragedy their nation was facing. There must have crossed through the minds of many there thoughts of a new leader rising on the horizon, a leader no one had heard about a short while back, Adolph Hitler with his brown-shirt followers. And a sense of foreboding fell upon the crowd.

"In a thousand different ways man has been persuaded to give up his natural relations with reality, and to seek his welfare in the magic formulas of some kind of economic and social witchcraft, by which the chance of freeing himself from economic and social misery is still further removed," the doctor said to them on that day.

The tragedy of this new kind of witchcraft, that of the leaders rising up in so many countries, in Germany, in Italy, in Russia, was, he told the audience, that a man was forced under them to give up his own material and spiritual personality, and live as one of the spiritually restless and materialistic masses which claimed control over him. He reminded them then of another Goethe celebration which would come in 1949, the two hundredth anniversary of the great poet's birth. But what would those next seventeen years bring? A sense of doom lay over the whole world then and no one knew when or where disaster would strike.

"May it be that he who gives the memorial address at that new festival will be able to state that the deep darkness which surrounds this one has already begun to lighten," the doctor went on. "That a race with a true feeling for reality is seeking to understand it and is beginning to achieve a mastery over material and social needs, united in its resolve to remain loyal to the one true ideal of humanity."

On his return from Europe to Africa, Dr. Schweitzer felt a deeper concern than he had felt on his first voyage, in 1913, before the first World War.

"With the spirit of the age, I am in complete disagreement because it is filled with disdain for thinking," he wrote.

There was not only disdain for thinking, but an actual distrust of it, he said. All the organized political, social and religious organizations of the time seemed to him to be trying to keep men from forming their own beliefs through their own thinking. They wanted the people to take as their own such ideas as they had ready made for them. Any man who actually did any thinking for himself was something inconvenient and even uncanny to these new leaders. The spirit of the age would not let a man discover his true self. And this thing that was happening would in time affect the whole world.

At his African hospital, Dr. Schweitzer could look out and see the silent Ogowe, with the same impenetrable forest, magnificently green, covering the island and the edge of the river on the opposite shore, mirrored in the dark water. Out there the monkeys leaped from tree to tree, the crocodiles slept on the sandbanks, the pelicans swooped low to skim the waters, as they had been doing since time began. Off in the darkness leopards roamed and elephants trampled close to their little banana plantations. The tsetse fly still flew out by day to bring sleeping sickness with its bite, and by night the mosquitoes kept up the attack.

Yet Africa, even as unchanged as she was, no longer was isolated from the world. Planes were flying now across the Atlantic and the Pacific. And planes could fly to Africa as well. When that time came, a journey through the jungles that took weeks by safari could be made in an hour or less. Boats, too, were faster than they had been in 1913, when the doctor first came here. The trip from Europe to Africa took only four weeks now. And mail arrived more often.

For the next seven years the doctor's time was divided between Africa and Europe, caring for the poor and sick or giving lectures and concerts in crowded halls, in the principal cities of Europe. His wife joined him often when he was in Africa and stayed as long as her health would permit. Then she would return to be with their daughter, in a cooler, drier climate.

To Dr. Schweitzer, home in Europe would always mean Günsbach, even after his father had died and the manse had others living in it. With the money he received for the Goethe award, he built a house in this little Alsatian village that held memories of a happy childhood. His fame had spread so that people came from many countries to call on him, whenever it was known that he was there.

There was a modesty about this man, unusual in a world gone power-mad, with bemedaled leaders strutting pompously before the people.

At sixty he had the same health and energy which in his youth had allowed him to study and write day and night without feeling fatigue.

"You can't go on burning your candle at both ends like this," a friend said to him once, after he had been working until four o'clock one morning.

"Oh, yes you can, if the candle is long enough," he answered.

He was a conscientious worker. Each lecture he gave was written out with painstaking care, then gone over sentence by sentence in advance, with an interpreter if he were to speak in a country where neither French nor German was understood. And before a concert he was known to practice as much as eight hours without a rest. With an assistant he would go many times up and down the stairs of an organ loft to get the effects of the various stops, because no two organs sound the same. Then he would pencil on the music the stops to be used, so the performance would be as perfect as he could make it.

Dr. Schweitzer was asked to preach the Christmas sermon once, in a town in Holland. Not only did he preach, but he played the organ as well. There was amazement on the faces of the people when they heard the prelude.

"Can this be our old organ?" they asked.

Without their knowing it, the doctor had spent several days in the organ loft, covered with dust and perspiration, cleaning the pipes himself.

There had been time, too, in his busy schedule, to bring out additional books, that had come slowly into existence, chapter by chapter. *The Mysticism of St. Paul the Apostle*,

Out of My Life and Thought and *The Great Thinkers of India.*

In 1939, when Dr. Schweitzer arrived in Europe for the regular visit he made every other year, it was to find the dread of war hanging like a dark cloud over all that part of the world. He decided to return immediately to Africa, without even waiting to unpack, in order to be sure that the sick of his hospital would not suffer for lack of medicines and supplies. A month later he was back on the Ogowe.

News came of the declaration of a war that had been so long expected. The doctor's wife and daughter had returned to Europe shortly before the news reached him, but he stayed on at his hospital. By taking in only the most urgent cases, and sending all who were not too seriously ill back to their own villages to be treated at home, the supply of drugs was enough to last at least two years.

The Africans who had been drafted to fight in the first World War had talked little about it after their return. There was a seriousness about them, as if the experience had weighed upon them so heavily they could not bring themselves to think of it.

"In the village the people ask me to tell them about the war, but I can't do it," one of the patients at the hospital had said to Dr. Schweitzer. "They wouldn't understand it if I did. It was all so horrible, so horrible."

Now in the second World War the horror was brought to Africa and the people saw it for themselves. The troops of General de Gaulle and the troops of Vichy fought for the possession of Lambaréné. The leaders of both sides gave orders to their men that the hospital, two and a half miles from the town, must not be bombed. But the walls of the buildings had to be reinforced with corrugated iron to protect them from the many stray shots that came that way.

With the victory of de Gaulle's men, the region was cut off

from France and the rest of Europe, but ships made their way now and then from America and England, to the West Coast of Africa.

Once when the supply of medicines for the hospital were almost gone, a gift came through from the people of America. Not only were there the much needed drugs, but there were other things, such as new cooking utensils for the kitchen, spectacles, shoes, powdered milk, cod-liver oil and other necessary vitamins. Again and again, as the crates were unpacked, there were exclamations of joy. Especially welcome was a pair of rubber gloves to fit the doctor's hands. For months past he had been wearing gloves too small for him when he had to perform operations.

Helene Schweitzer managed to return by way of Portugal and a roundabout way through the Portuguese and Belgian colonies of Africa, to help her husband. And four faithful nurses as well remained all during the war.

When word came of the war's end in Europe, it was during the hour of repose, after the noon meal. Dr. Schweitzer was sitting at his table writing some important letters that had to make the river boat by two o'clock. A European, who had been listening to a portable radio, came bringing the news to him. The doctor finished his letters, then went down to the hospital wards where he was needed. It was not until evening that he could allow himself to stop and think of what the end of fighting in Europe meant. The hospital bell had been rung to spread the good news, and there was rejoicing among the staff and patients. But the doctor, alone in his room, took from the shelf his little book with the sayings of Lao-tse, the great Chinese thinker who had lived more than twenty-five centuries before. A gentle breeze rustled the palms outside his window, while he sat quietly reading.

"Weapons are disastrous implements, no tools for a noble being. Only he who cannot do otherwise, does he make use of them. Quiet and peace are for him the highest. He conquers, but knows no joy in it. He who would rejoice in victory would be rejoicing in murder. At the celebration of victory, the general should take his place as is the custom at funeral ceremonies. The slaughter of human beings in great numbers should be lamented with tears of compassion. Therefore should he, who has conquered in battle, bear himself as if he were at a festival of mourning."

After ten years in Africa without a rest or change of climate, Dr. Schweitzer joined his family at last in the Black Forest of Germany, and then in Switzerland, where there were four grandchildren waiting to greet him.

His fame had been spreading steadily during the years. Not only the musicians and the learned men whose interests lay in philosophy or theology, but a whole war-weary world felt the need of the message he had to give.

"The fundamental idea of good is thus, that it consists in preserving life, in favoring it, in wanting to bring it to its highest value. And evil consists in destroying life, doing it injury, hindering its development."

The people from countries outside of Europe began asking him to come to them. Requests came from America, Australia and from the Orient. In 1949 Dr. Schweitzer accepted an invitation to speak at Aspen, Colorado, for the two hundredth anniversary of Goethe's birth. Crowds came from all over the country to the little western American town to hear him. As he spoke in his native tongue, an interpreter repeated his words, sentence by sentence.

For many in the audience there was such a complete communion of spirit that they seemed to follow his meaning, not through the interpreter alone, but through the words he spoke himself, in a tongue unknown to them.

"Yes, it often happens that way between people of different languages," Dr. Schweitzer said, when one in the audience told him later about it. "I have found that understanding many times between the natives of Africa and myself, without the need of words."

Few men can resist the temptations of the adulation and riches that go with fame. But Dr. Schweitzer chose to return quietly to his hospital in Africa to carry on the work he had started. There was even an attitude of surprise and wonder that this had happened to him. Letters came in by the thousands through the little post office at Lambaréné. The doctor, in his humility, was touched by this tribute, and he tried to answer them all himself, though it meant working until late in the night by the light of an oil lamp.

One evening in the fall of 1953, a young assistant came to the room where Dr. Schweitzer was busy writing, and interrupted him to tell of what he had just heard over his portable radio. The Nobel prize for peace, for the previous year, had just been awarded the doctor. He received the news in silence. He put down his pen and covered his face with his hands, without saying a word.

The lepers of this part of Africa were the ones who benefited from this honor. The money that came with the award, with an equal amount added by the country of Norway, was spent in building a model village on the hill above the hospital, to house the three hundred leper patients. With modern medicines, all can be cured and eventually returned to their villages. But during the convalescence and the period of observation after, they have firm, well-built houses to live in. And there is a modern room for examination and treatment.

Chapter XIV

Happy are those to whom the years of work are allotted in richer measure than those seeking and waiting! Happy those who in the end are able to give themselves really and completely!

Out of My Life and Thought

AMONG THE PASSENGERS of a train going to London from the English Channel, on a day in October, 1955, there sat a quiet man, with a white mustache and that slight stoop to his shoulders that comes from sitting long hours at a desk. His neat black suit was carelessly worn, as if it had been forgotten as soon as it had been put on. And when he took off his hat, his white hair fell straggling over his forehead. When he spoke to his companions, it was in German, but with an accent that was soft, without the usual thick, guttural sounds.

Glancing casually at him, any other third-class passenger would easily have accepted him as one of his own kind, and would have gone back to reading his newspaper or looking out the window at the swiftly moving landscape.

The train pulled in at the London station and the white-haired man gathered up his well-worn luggage with an energy which showed a spirit of youth. As he stepped off the train, the other passengers who had lingered behind looked on in astonishment, to see this unobtrusive man surrounded by reporters and photographers, who had rushed down the platform from the place where the first-class coaches had stopped. They flashed their cameras and asked questions, writing the answers in their notebooks. Who was this man, who had ridden so quietly with them in the third-class compartment? Some of the other passengers, who had looked more closely, might have remembered an expression in his eyes, combined with a strength and intelligence, a kindness and gentleness of manner, that set him apart from others.

Dr. Schweitzer had arrived in London to receive the Order of Merit, the highest honor of the land, bestowed on him by Queen Elizabeth. The only other living person not a citizen of Great Britain ever to receive this honor was President Dwight D. Eisenhower.

When it had been announced that Albert Schweitzer would visit London, the finest hotels had been eager to have him as a guest, but he chose to stay at the home of an old friend from Alsace, whom he had known in his youth. The friend had a tearoom in London, and when the news spread that Dr. Schweitzer was staying there people crowded in to pay him homage.

Among many others, Bertrand Russell, the philosopher, came. And Augustus John, the artist, realized one of his most cherished ambitions, when he was able to meet the doctor and draw a portrait of him.

"Sat like a brick, he did," was the artist's comment on the much-interrupted sitting, when he was asked about it by reporters.

On the nineteenth of October, the Ambassador of France drove up to the little tearoom in a gleaming black limousine to take the doctor with him to Buckingham Palace, where the award was to be made.

When the official ceremonies were over, the young Queen sat talking with Dr. Schweitzer, eager to hear about his work among the natives of Africa.

There was a luncheon later with the Prime Minister, Sir Anthony Eden. And the University of Cambridge conferred on Dr. Schweitzer an honorary degree of Doctor of Law. In his speech of presentation, given in Latin, the Public Orator said:

"He could certainly have attained the highest honors in the learned world, had he not preferred to follow the call of his Lord and ours, listening to the voice of Him who bade his disciples to heal the sick, cleanse the lepers and freely give as they had freely received. Let us by all means, as befits a University, praise the great physician, honor a distinguished writer, and express our thanks to an inspired interpreter of music. But in all humility, let us salute this faithful soldier of Christ, seeing in him an example of Christian charity long to be remembered."

This tribute was made to the man who, throughout the years, had remained true to his schoolboy resolution not to let himself "grow ripe with age," never to be ashamed of the dreams of his youth. At eighty, Dr. Schweitzer had the same ideals and enthusiasms he had had as a boy, when he had looked with compassion on an old horse being led to slaughter, and when he had scattered the birds to protect them from the stones of his companion. At eighty, he still refused to set himself above other men, just as he had refused, at five, to wear clothes the village boys could not afford to wear.

Certain responsibilities were bound to come with fame such as his. Whenever he was at his home in Günsbach it was not the quiet little village it was at other times. As soon as it became known that he had arrived from Africa, crowds of people began coming into the village on pilgrimages to see and talk to him.

"You shouldn't try to see them all," his friends often urged him. "You must save your strength."

But with his typical Alsatian stubbornness, the doctor refused to listen to them. He would let no one be turned away. Automobiles, taxis, motorcycles, bicycles, were parked outside his door that opened on the street leading from Günsbach to Münster. Some had come from long distances just to have a glimpse of this great man. The Queen Mother of Belgium came to pay her visit, as she did each time he returned to Europe. Mme. Pandit from India came. Doctors, musicians, university professors, heads of governments, students on Fulbright fellowships from America, tourists who had read his works or heard his concerts in halls or on phonograph records, all came.

Peasants and villagers, scholars and humble workmen, he insisted upon seeing them all. Known and unknown, they came all during the day, some in need of help and some to bring simple gifts of flowers or fruit.

There was something about him that gave each one he talked with some feeling of importance when the interview was over. It was as if each person alone had been singled out above all the others, and the doctor had taken a special interest in the things he said and did.

After a visit of six months in Europe, the doctor began to make plans to return to his hospital in Africa. The last of the buildings in the leper village were almost finished and he wanted to see how they were getting on. And the brush needed to be cleared away from the fruit orchard which the jungle was ever trying to claim for its own once more. There were the sick, too, who still came to the hospital. Every day the canoes were paddled up to the landing, with the well bringing in their sick. Some limped up the slope with painful sores, some came staggering with wounds received in a fight or from some savage beast. Mothers brought their babies, burning with a fever and tied securely and tenderly on their backs. There were still the orphans and the homeless old ones.

How many journeys throughout the years he had made up the Ogowe River from the West Coast of Africa. Sometimes he arrived by day at his destination, when he could stand on deck with eyes searching eagerly along the palm-bordered

banks for a first glimpse of Lambaréné. The sun would spar-
kle like sequins on the waves, and now and then a fish would
leap up, a flash of silver, then disappear. Or a lead-colored
watersnake would go gliding by, indifferent to all around it.
Canoes, carved out of hollow logs, would pass up and down,
undisturbed now by hippopotamuses or crocodiles except in
remote places where the villages lie far apart.

At other times it was late at night when, with a blast of its
whistle, the boat pulled up to the landing place at Lambaréné. Then one by one the lights would appear in houses and
trading stores, and people would gather at the water's edge.
Here and there in the little native villages between the town
and the hospital there might be heard the sound of tomtoms
beating a message which many of the older people still understood. "The canoe that brings the Grand Doctor is coming
this way."

The Christmas of 1955 was spent on the steamer between
Bordeaux and Port Gentil. The large green wreath that had
hung above the dining table at the hospital had been taken
down, dry and brittle, with the candles burned to their ends,
by the time the doctor arrived at the hospital. There was another celebration soon to follow, however. On January 14,
Dr. Schweitzer's eighty-first birthday was celebrated in many
parts of the world with lectures, concerts or sermons. But at
the hospital at Lambaréné the celebration was the same as for
the birthdays of all the other members of the staff.

At half past seven, just before the gong for breakfast
sounded, Dr. Schweitzer's co-workers gathered outside his
door. Like long-stemmed walking mushrooms, with their
white clothes and large white helmets, they came from all
directions. They walked from the hospital wards where the
doctors and nurses had been at work since the first bell rang
at sunrise, from the leper village, from the outside kitchen,
the linen room and from the garden patch by the riverbank.

They sang songs to wish him a happy birthday. Then they went into his room to shake his hand.

It was a small room and could not hold them all at the same time. Like every other room for staff and guests, it was plain and simply furnished. The floors were bare and the straight wooden chairs were cushionless. There was a mosquito net draped over the iron cot, and two tables in the room were piled high with work waiting to be done. Through an open door the metal-lined piano could be seen at one end of a small anteroom, and at the other end the pen for the baby antelopes.

The doctor and his staff went off together to the big dining hall across the courtyard. A semicircle of green branches decorated the doctor's place at the center of the long table. Two lighted candles nestled among the branches, and around the plate were piled gifts from the staff. They were simple gifts, as the doctor's life was simple, the kind that could be made during spare hours or bought at the trading stores of Lambaréné.

"But come," the doctor said, when the gifts had been unwrapped, and each one had been thanked in turn. This was a Saturday and there was work to be done. They ate their breakfast of bread, leavened with bananas and baked in the brick oven in the kitchen. There was jam made from the tropical fruit grown on the place, and for a special treat there was tinned butter which had been sent from Denmark and powdered milk from America to go with the African coffee.

At eight o'clock the bell rang again. It was the time for roll call and the division of labor. There were new faces that had not been here six months before when the doctor had left for Europe. And others were missing, for the workers were recruited from those who had come to stay with some sick member of their family or tribe, or from the patients themselves who had recovered enough to do light labor.

"M'bolo, Docteur," they called out to him with broad smiles.

The courtyard scene had changed little throughout the years. Dogs, cats and black and white African ducks pecked in the damp earth in search of worms. Parrots whistled and called out words in the different languages they had heard, and a young chimpanzee turned somersaults and swung on the porch rails like a mischievous child. The antelopes put their moist black noses through the wire of their pen, looking on in curiosity.

Some who had been at the hospital longer than others went quietly about their given tasks. They wore neat khaki shorts and blue denim shirts and aprons, with only a bandaged ankle or wrist to show that they had once come as patients. But among those lately come, there was a show of bewilderment. It would take time for them to adjust to the routine.

There was the same colorful array of garments of every description as there had been in the beginning of the hospital's existence, the gay prints of Manchester cloth wrapped in folds around the body, the cast-off clothes, now in tatters, the loincloths on the almost naked bodies of those from the deep interior. The faces of some were tattooed with tribal marks, and many had sharpened teeth with one broken off in the middle.

A name was called and there was an answer of "Wuh" as each in turn stepped forward. Some took hoes and went off to work in the vegetable patch, others took axes and machetes to cut away the ever creeping underbrush. Some helped in the building, the painting, the repairing or cleaning. And for some there were easy tasks that could be done sitting down, such as weaving bamboo shades to protect the seedlings in the garden from sun and rain.

The doctor turned away and went down to the hospital wards. Here, too, there were new faces that had not been at the hospital six months ago, new patients taking the place of those who had recovered and returned to their villages. They lay on their beds, bearing the fever and the pain with that patience and endurance that all creatures living close to nature have learned. The doctor went from bed to bed, with words of comfort for each one, and with his quick, experienced eye he knew how much hope there was.

He passed the nursery with its neat white wall hangings of muslin, decorated by one of the nurses with drawings of elephants, monkeys and giraffes. From three bassinets, three pairs of wide black eyes stared up at him, and chubby little legs kicked and pawed the air contentedly. These were the orphaned babies who were being given a healthy, secure start in life.

Joseph was now back at the hospital, though no longer as a worker. He had a room to himself down near the river where he could look across the channel to the Galoa village that had once been his home. Though he was younger than the doctor, his days of usefulness were over. The wife he had saved for for so long, was dead, and his children were all grown and married. The money he had received for his daughters had long since been spent, and his son had a family of his own to think about.

He had come to spend his last years at the one place where he knew he would be taken in and cared for.

Oyembo had returned earlier as a patient, but as soon as he was well again he had gone back to his village by the lake. The friendship between him and the doctor had continued through the years.

There were other old friends who greeted Dr. Schweitzer when he climbed the hill to the leper village, for here the patients stayed longer to make sure the disease did not recur.

"M'bolo, Docteur," "Bon jour, Docteur," could be heard from every side.

What a pleasure it was to see them living in well-constructed buildings, protected against the rain and the tropical sun. They had a look of pride and self-assurance one does not find in the villages where the people sleep on no other bed than a mat of woven straw spread on a dirt floor, with snakes and insects crawling in, and the night rains seeping through.

The finishing touches were being put on the last of the buildings. The doctor made his tour of inspection, stepping from place to place as briskly as any man half his age.

A group of children had been practicing their songs. Led by their Pahouin teacher and Mama Helene, they came trooping down the hill to the windows of the dining hall during the noon meal, to serenade the Grand Docteur on his birthday. Their childish voices sang out the old familiar tunes of Europe, with the short, staccato words of their own language.

An hour of repose followed the meal, then work was taken up again as always. M'bulu, who interprets the Sunday sermons for the Galoas, came up from the boat landing with sacks of mail he had brought from the Lambaréné post office. But the doctor was off in the orchards or working in the leper village, or among the patients in the hospital wards. It was not until the evening bell was rung that he could call his time his own.

The day ends as quickly as it begins, near the Equator. As soon as the sun sinks behind the trees on the western horizon, lean, gray parrots with bright red tail feathers go squawking and whistling back to their roosting places. The weaver birds flock to the leafy branches of the cinnamon tree, and the water birds nestle on the papyrus islands, giving a sleepy chirp now and then. There is a moment of brilliant color in the sky, orange and fiery red and gold reflected in a sparkling band on the water. Then darkness falls suddenly. The cicadas and frogs and flying dogs take up their chirps and croaks and clacking calls where they had left off at dawn, and the shivering cry of an owl or the screech of a monkey joins in from time to time.

All along the corridors of the long, low hospital buildings, cooking fires glowed like pumpkin jack-o'-lanterns where families of the patients prepared their evening meal. There was a steady chatter, some laughed, some called out in angry words, and some sang a native song, with notes first high then low as a bird sings. Now and then a baby cried or someone coughed, or from the wards inside there was a groan of pain.

The oil lamps were lit in the dining hall and Dr. Schweitzer met with his staff for the evening meal. There were some faithful assistants who had been with him for many years, returning to the hospital again and again after a leave of absence in their own countries. There were others, young and idealistic, turning their backs on material success as Dr. Schweitzer himself had done almost half a century ago. Perhaps not all would remain, but their lives would be richer for this experience whatever the future held for them.

Back in his room, in the quiet of the tropical night, Dr. Schweitzer looked over the cablegrams and letters that had come from people all over the world. Every letter brought new proof of the truth in the words he had written long ago.

"Our humanity is by no means so materialistic as foolish talk is continually asserting it to be."

The curfew bell rang at nine o'clock. The doctors and nurses who happened still to be in the dining hall, left quietly for their own rooms. The last to go blew out the lamps and locked the door. Outside, the fires of the cooking pots had been extinguished with the ringing of the bell, and the noisy palavers had come to a sudden end. A gentle wind caused the lamplight in the doctor's room to flicker, and the mango trees swayed with a murmuring sound. A little kid gave a bleat like a baby's cry and was answered by a reassuring call from the mother goat. Tchu-tchu, the white and yellow dog, lay curled at his master's feet, deep in dreams of the chase.

"With calmness and humility I look forward to the future `..."

It had been twenty-five years ago that Dr. Schweitzer wrote these words. Now at eighty-one, as he worked on, reading and answering letters, or taking up the book which he was writing, his ears were alert. A sound on the river might mean a canoe coming to the landing with someone needing care, a step on the walk might mean a message that he was needed down in the hospital ward.

"Whether we be workers or sufferers, it is assuredly our duty to conserve our powers as being men who have won through to the peace which passeth all understanding."

Bibliography

Anderson, Erica. *The World of Albert Schweitzer*, A Book of Photographs. New York: Harper & Brothers, 1955

Dorny, Andre. *Legends d'Alsace*. Paris: Librairie Istra, 1954

Feschotte, Jacques. *Albert Schweitzer*. Boston: Beacon Press, 1955

Livingstone, David. *The Last Journals of David Livingstone*. New York: Harper & Brothers, 1875

Marthelot, Pierre; Dollinger, Philippe; Heitz, Robert; Biedermann, Alfred. *Visages de l'Alsace*. Paris: Editions Horizons de France, 1948

Schmitt, Ernest. *Le Beau Val St. Gregoire en Alsace, La Vallée de Münster*. Strasbourg: F. L. Le Roux, 1945

Schweitzer, Albert. *Christianity and the Religions of the World*. New York: Macmillan Co., 1951

———. "The Ethics of the Reverence for Life." New York: *Christendom*

———. *Goethe*. London: Adam & Charles Black, 1949

———. *Histoires de la Forêt Vierge*. Paris: Payot, 1941

———. *Indian Thought and Its Development*. New York: Henry Holt, 1936

———. *Jean Sebastien Bach*. New York: Macmillan Co., 1950

———. *Memoirs of Childhood and Youth*. New York: Macmillan Co., 1949

———. *On the Edge of the Primeval Forest. More from the Primeval Forest*. New York: Macmillan Co., 1952

———. *Out of My Life and Thought*. New York: Henry Holt & Co., 1949

———. *Paul and His Interpreters.* New York: Macmillan Co., 1951

———. *The Philosophy of Civilization.* New York: Macmillan Co., 1949

———. *The Quest of the Historical Jesus.* New York: Macmillan Co., 1948

Sittler, Lucien. *Histoire d'Alsace.* Colmar: Editions Alsatia, 1951

Smith, E. W. *African Ideas of God.* London: Edinburgh House Press, 1950

Ward, Herbert. *A Voice from the Congo.* London: William Heinemann, 1910

Index

INDEX

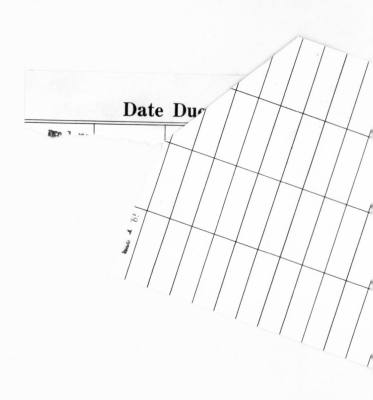

Date Due